7 Paths

to

MANAGERIAL LEADERSHIP

Doing Well by Doing It Right

Fred Mackenzie

PRESS

ATD Press is an internationally renowned source of insightful and practical
information on talent development, workplace learning, and professional
development.

ATD Press
1640 King Street
Alexandria, VA 22314 USA

Ordering information: Books published by ATD Press can be purchased by visiting
ATD's website at www.td.org/books or by calling 800.628.2783 or 703.683.8100.

Library of Congress Control Number: 2015961039

ISBN-10: 1-56286-945-0
ISBN-13: 978-1-56286-945-8
e-ISBN: 978-1-60728-280-8

ATD Press Editorial Staff
Director: Kristine Luecker
Manager: Christian Green
Community of Practice Manager, Management: Ryan Changcoco
Developmental Editor: Kathryn Stafford
Text Design: Maggie Hyde and Iris Sanchez
Cover Design: Iris Sanchez
Printed by Total Printing Systems, Newton, IL

To Nancy R. Lee
Enlightened scholar and steadfast supporter
without whom this book would never have been written.

Contents

Introduction

This book is for you, the manager and supervisor of others. There are many good books on management, ranging from strategic planning to decision making. There has been, as well, a steady stream of insightful books on leadership, describing those attributes necessary for inspiring others to have confidence in you, the leader. This book is about managerial leadership: the art of getting exceptional work done through the willing efforts of others. It focuses on action, not position, to inspire others to have confidence in themselves. The 7 Paths approach in this book is a middle management presentation of the work of Nancy R. Lee (*The Practice of Managerial Leadership*, 2007) and Elliott Jaques (*Requisite Organization: A Total System for Effective Managerial Organization and Managerial Leadership for the 21st Century*, 2006). *7 Paths to Managerial Leadership* has been inspired by their work and ideas, as has my own career as a manager, consultant, teacher, and counselor. The case study examples describing each path are derived from my more than 25 years of experience both as a senior manager and as a consultant advising organizations and their managers.

The organization of this book is as follows: In chapter 1, the organizational significance of the middle manager–direct report relationship is introduced, and the four leadership styles common to most middle managers are described. Chapter 2 discusses how the 7 Paths improve work behavior for both employees and managers by presenting new approaches, processes, and procedures. Chapter 3 presents Path 1, managerial planning and task assignment—the basis for team success—and details the specifics of any task: what by when. In chapter 4, Path 2 covers the importance of regular, effective, and purposeful meetings. Chapter 5 presents Path 3, context setting, which is a manager's opportunity to offer the organizational picture for direct reports. In chapter 6, Path 4 details how to offer positive and constructive recognition to team members. Chapter 7, Path 5, discusses the dos and don'ts of performance appraisals, and chapter 8, Path 6, examines how best to coach direct reports for optimum growth within their roles. Lastly, chapter 9 presents Path 7, how best to integrate continual improvement into the manager's role.

Additionally, there are several appendices helpful for guiding middle managers in the day-to-day supervisory functions of their jobs—for example, describing how to establish key accountabilities and write clear task assignments. For the big picture, Appendix E, Making Strategy Work—The Linkage Process, further explains the relationship between individual efforts and an organization's short- and long-term goals.

1

Managers and Their Direct Reports: A Dynamic Relationship

You may remember your first role as a manager of others, as someone who gets work done through the efforts of other people. You were probably promoted because of your excellence as an individual contributor–you got your work done! And perhaps upper management thought you had an above-average "feel" for working with others. However, managing others is more than getting along; it involves deciding who can do the work, who needs coaching on specific assignments, who can be left alone to accomplish a task, and who needs role development. All managers carry this managerial leadership accountability.

According to the renowned organizational scientist Elliott Jaques, "managerial teamworking is the most powerful leadership enhancing mechanism of all. In effective teamworking, the strength of the mutual influencing between a manager and a subordinate reaches its highest level; context setting and mutual understanding are at their clearest. There is an immediate sharing of values, and the result is the greatest possibility of maximum commitment by all to the achievement of commonly valued goals."

Middle Management Styles

Managerial leadership combines the discipline of managing a unit with the skill of allowing direct reports to work at their level of capability, grow in their roles, and produce extraordinary results. It focuses on managers reaching their full potential and, at the same time, inspiring members of their teams to do the same. This, in turn, increases the effectiveness of the total organization.

There are four leadership styles common to most middle managers (Figure 1-1). First are those managers who are high on managerial skills but lack the people orientation to allow direct reports to be self-motivated (Impoverished Managing). They tend to micromanage their teams and seek perfection. Feedback is generally negative, and there is little managerial coaching.

The second group includes those who are optimistic, inspirational, and wonderful to be around (Contagious Enthusiasm). Their interpersonal skills are great, and people follow their direction; however, their planning, organizing, implementing, and evaluating skills are lacking. This often happens when a person is promoted from a successful

Figure 1-1: Middle Management Styles

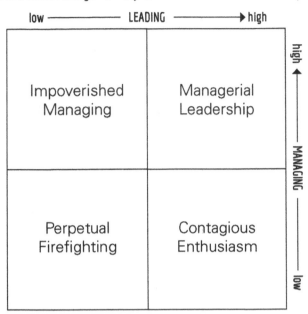

low ——————— LEADING ——————→ high

Impoverished Managing	Managerial Leadership
Perpetual Firefighting	Contagious Enthusiasm

high ↑ MANAGING ↓ low

individual contributor to a managerial position without the necessary management training.

The third group represents those individuals who have little or no skills in either leadership or management (Perpetual Firefighting). These people exist as managers, but usually not for long. Their work-day involves putting out fires, planning for contingencies, and trying to survive. They work hard but make little progress.

The fourth group includes middle managers who combine their managerial skills with the understanding and practice of involving their direct reports in the goals of the unit (Managerial Leadership). Their vocabulary includes such words as *participation, empowerment, enablement, growth, context setting,* and *collaboration.* As a unit, they meet or exceed their goals. All managers are somewhere along the LEADING scale and somewhere along the MANAGING scale. Which is your primary window—the one from which you see the world of work?

When the key elements of highly successful organizations are examined, an effective middle manager-direct report relationship stands out as one of the foundational links in getting work done. Strategies, long-range plans, and corporate objectives are all important, but the cascading of accountabilities and task assignments to the operational level is what results in work output. This relationship must be clear, honest, trusting, and continuous. It is a major part of every manager's job. The most important relationship in a managerial hierarchy is that of a manager and a direct report. Managers are held accountable not only for doing their best personally but also for the results of the work and the working behavior of those in their workforce.

Have you ever had a manager like this?

> "Welcome to the unit. I am your manager, and I will be laying out the work I expect you to do. Don't argue with me. If you have a question, ask someone in the unit. Don't bring me problems. I expect you to solve them yourself. If you do well, we'll get along. If you don't get done what I expect, I'll get someone else to replace you. Do I make myself clear?"

Or this?

> "Welcome to the unit. I am your manager, and I have written out a list of things you and I will be working on. Read it over and jot down any questions you may have.

Let's get together tomorrow morning at 9 to finalize the list and put some completion dates down. Now, I'd like to take you around to meet your colleagues, who will help you get oriented. It's good to have you onboard."

Exit interview studies have indicated that most people do not leave an organization because they dislike the organization; they leave because they do not like their manager and the way they are supervised. Results of a Gallup survey on manager-employee engagement revealed that "among employees who strongly agree that their manager helps them set performance goals, 69 percent are engaged. When employees strongly disagree, just 8 percent are engaged, while 53 percent are actively disengaged" (Harter and Adkins 2015).

Developing Effective Relationships

This book is based on seven approaches to the development of an effective relationship between middle managers and their direct reports. The 7 Paths to Managerial Leadership are as follows:

1. Managerial Planning and Task Assignment
2. Managerial Meetings
3. Context Setting
4. Feedback
5. Performance Appraisal
6. Coaching Direct Reports
7. Continual Improvement

These 7 Paths contain practices that are based on sound, proven principles covering decades of evaluation and fine-tuning. Simply stated, they determine:

- tasks that need to be accomplished
- feedback to team members
- evaluation of the work obtained.

My experience applying these principles as a manager has shown that direct reports like the way the paths become productive work practices. In turn, this positive attitude and behavior lead to a motivated and productive work unit.

Once you review the 7 Paths, select the ones that go with the grain of your thinking and start implementing those. Once you've begun, revisit the remaining paths and select one or more to experiment with. In time, you may find that all the practices are helpful as you develop a high-performing team to be proud of. Becoming a competent managerial leader will result in less firefighting, less overtime work, and an overall reduction of your stress level.

The paths are sequenced in the order they usually occur. The first, Managerial Planning and Task Assignment, is probably the most detailed to apply, but this path is the core of any management system. This is an excellent place to start. Spending some time improving where you are as "a manager of others" instead of pondering where you should be will be the key to your continued success.

Leo Tolstoy wrote, "Everyone thinks of changing the world, but no one thinks of changing himself." This book will help you change yourself as a manager. Read it with a pencil handy.

Checklist for an Effective Middle Manager–Direct Report Relationship

☑ Keep discussions on an adult-to-adult basis, not parent to child.
☑ Promote mutual trust through openness and clarity.

☑ Exercise managerial leadership, not managerial dictatorship.

☑ Encourage feedback from your team.

☑ Remember that this is a two-way working relationship.

☑ Work toward a continuous and dynamic relationship.

2

Why 7 Paths?

The 7 Paths approach is an effective way to combat an unconscious false assumption that managers have been making for decades: that, given clear assignments, direct reports will produce precisely what the manager expects.

Organizational Structure

Every organization starts with an idea, a purpose, and a plan. Based on this plan, an organization structure is put together. This structure is composed of roles or positions showing what roles report directly to the CEO or president, what roles report to certain senior positions, and so on. Staffing follows, placing people in the roles who are judged capable of doing the work of the role.

It is assumed that if the assignments in a role are clear and there is an individual who has the necessary qualifications to fill the role, then that person will complete the work as specified and the organization will receive the results expected.

In real life, this assumption does not always turn out to be true. Over and over again, managers are heard to say, "We are not getting the results we should be getting given the people and resources we have."

Human Forces Filter

There is an assumed sequence to work output (Figure 2-1). However, there is a fundamental reason why this sequence does not automatically happen (Figure 2-2).

Figure 2-1: Work Output Sequence

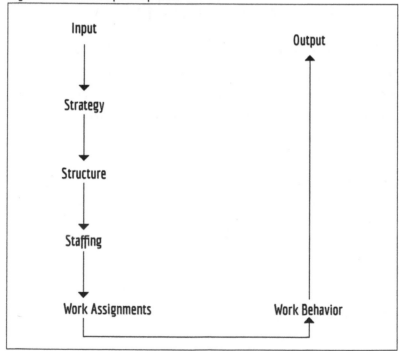

Input → Strategy → Structure → Staffing → Work Assignments → Work Behavior → Output

Figure 2-2: Work Output and Individual Influences

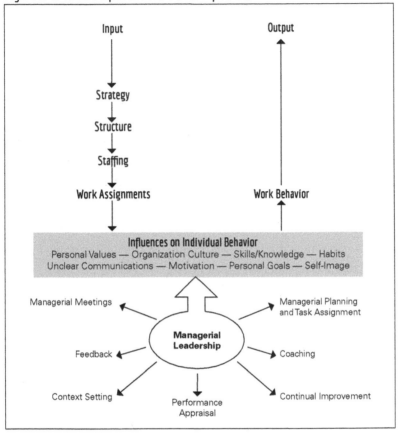

A person's behavior toward a given goal goes through a filter that influences the work output. It is called the Human Forces Filter. This filter is different for each employee and includes such things as:

- work values developed over time
- organization culture
- person's relationship with manager

- skills and knowledge individual has (or does not have)
- habits acquired over time
- individual goals at any given time
- what is understood or not understood about assignments
- what actually motivates the individual
- self-image.

Employees' work behavior is affected by their unique prism, often resulting in a somewhat different output from what was expected by the manager. *7 Paths to Managerial Leadership* presents ways to ameliorate these individual differences. Meaningful new approaches, processes, and procedures are presented, which, when they are implemented and become habits, will result in improved work behavior for both managers and their direct reports. Following these paths will:

- Replace bad habits with good habits.
- Build teamwork.
- Involve direct reports in unit thinking.
- Clarify task assignments that must be done.
- Allow for mature (adult-to-adult) dialogue.
- Foster individual growth.
- Facilitate improvement through proper coaching.
- Ensure ongoing performance effectiveness.
- Utilize both positive and constructive feedback.

It is not the intention of using the 7 Paths to change an employee's personality, individual values, or personal goals. The objective is to enable improvement and growth of the direct report, help build the team, maintain a stimulating environment, and produce outstanding results. That is managerial leadership.

This approach is not an overnight solution. It is a journey that develops managerial leadership. It is a guide for managers to improve their practices in three areas:

1. defining the individual tasks that need to be accomplished
2. providing ongoing feedback to team members
3. evaluating the results of task completion.

Start with one path, then another. You will find the process a powerful and refreshing experience for you and your staff.

3

Path 1: Managerial Planning and Task Assignment

Managers plan what has to be done in their unit, by whom, by when, and how best to use available resources. To do this requires a clear vision of what has to be done, how to carry out the manager's role, and how to communicate it to the team.

Managerial Planning

Managers complete a task in three ways:

1. They do it themselves.
2. They complete it with the help of a direct report.
3. They delegate it to a direct report.

When defining tasks for a direct report, there are four things for a manager to specify: 1) quantity, 2) quality, 3) completion time, and 4) available resources (QQTR). A task can be defined as a "what by when." Managers should encourage team members to participate in the task assignment process by providing input, detailing possible action steps, and examining various approaches to task completion. However, the manager makes the final work-planning decisions. When delegating a task, the manager should enable staff to report back when conditions have changed and there is a possibility of the assignment not being completed to QQTR.

This is a good time to rate yourself on how well you are presently planning the work in your unit. Put an X anywhere along the scale where you believe best describes your present performance (Figure 3-1).

Figure 3-1: Self-Assessment for Managerial Planning

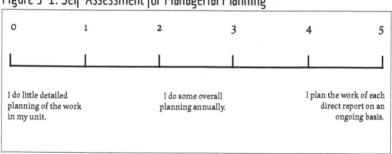

Who Is Accountable?

Have you ever experienced a situation like this?

John: Hey Joe, how are you coming along on the procedure manual for the new copy machine assembly line?

Joe: I've given it to Ted to do, John, but he has been very busy with his regular work. I'll check into it and let you know.

John: Well, you recall I mentioned it to you a couple of weeks ago. My boss says he wants to show it to the VPs next month at the big meeting.

Joe: I don't think we can get it done that fast, John, with vacations and all. Helen has been out on maternity leave, and I'm not sure when she's coming back. As you know, Ted is doing some of Helen's work.

John: I don't want excuses, Joe—this is a high priority for my boss, and I'll be in trouble if we don't produce. And you know what that means!

The first step in managerial planning is to be clear about what is expected from your managerial role. Specifically,

- What are you accountable for?
- What unit, functional, or departmental goals are assigned to you?
- What resources (people or funds, for example) do you have?

Without clarity, anything you do can be misdirected and, unfortunately, in the end, unappreciated. Your manager may not be used to giving you clear, specific goals with appropriate resources, but this information is essential to your ongoing success. At the beginning of a work cycle, one or more frank discussions with your manager clarifying your accountabilities are a must. Good managers have clear purpose.

There's a German proverb—"What's the use of running if you are not on the right path?"—that underscores the importance of both clarity and direction.

As a manager, you have the accountability to get certain things accomplished beyond what you can physically do yourself. That's why you have a team to help you. It's your job to set out "who is going to do what." In other words, the work-planning process consists of determining what has to be done and which employee is able to complete which assignment.

The process of managerial planning also includes the accountability for building an effective ongoing team, taking into consideration:

- Who needs specific coaching to complete a new task?
- Who needs development in a current role?
- Who is ready and willing to take on more responsibility?

Manager's Checklist

Successful managers:

☑ Plan how to accomplish the work of their units.

☑ Make the work-planning decisions for their units.

☑ Discuss work-planning options with their direct reports whenever possible and seek their suggestions.

Action Plan

Review your completed self-assessment (Figure 3-1). List some possible action plans you would like to implement during the next six months regarding your managerial planning. Here are some examples:

- Generate a list of tasks that you are working on that could possibly be delegated (or partially delegated) to one or more of your direct reports, with the list to be completed by a designated date.

- By (date), conduct a meeting with all direct reports for the purpose of getting feedback as to how well your planning of the unit's work is functioning, including suggestions for how it might be improved.
- By (date), review the completion dates of all direct reports' task assignments and prepare a schedule of informal discussions with each individual as to the progress being made.

Task Assignment

There are two types of assignments contained in any role. The first are the specific tasks assigned to the role. The second are general responsibilities assigned to the role.

Some organizations combine the two under the heading "Role Accountabilities." By listing the high-priority items (perhaps four to six for each type), focus can then be directed to what are called key accountabilities, which are those that comprise the most important work to be done and, hence, the most important factors for the performance appraisal. Key accountabilities, key specific task assignments, and the key general responsibilities typically account for about 80 percent of the effort of the individual in the role.

Often, when an employee's accomplishments are lagging behind expectations it is because of lack of clarity. Clear task assignments are the core of any management system. They are central to building trust within the organization.

As you did for managerial planning, rate yourself on how well you are assigning tasks in your unit (Figure 3-2).

Figure 3-2: Self-Assessment: Task Assignment

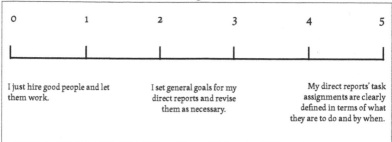

| 0 | 1 | 2 | 3 | 4 | 5 |

I just hire good people and let them work.

I set general goals for my direct reports and revise them as necessary.

My direct reports' task assignments are clearly defined in terms of what they are to do and by when.

Specific Tasks

The person who starts out going nowhere in particular generally gets there. —Dale Carnegie

A specific task is an assignment to produce a desired result within a time-frame during which quality, quantity, and resources are prescribed. It has three parts: the verb, which denotes closure; the subject; and the completion date.

Table 3-1: Examples of Task Assignments

Closure Verb	Subject	Completion Date
Complete	proposal for revised vacation plan	by 7/31
Submit	recommendations for an onboarding program	by 8/31
Reduce	avoidable turnover by 10 percent compared with average for years 20xx-20yy	by 12/31
Increase	by 15 percent customer satisfaction ratings over last year	by 1/2
Achieve	profit of minimum $200K from products and services projects	by 12/31

Closure Verb	Subject	Completion Date
Provide	up-to-date budget information to chief accountant for use in budget consolidation	monthly beginning 1/31
Conduct	three customer relations workshops for new salespeople	by 7/1
Establish	a security procedure for after-hours entry into building	by 4/30
Generate	a draft policy for relocation expenses	by 9/1
Identify	four possible store locations in Ohio	by 1/1

When writing a specific task assignment, begin the sentence with a verb that describes closure, not just an activity. For example, use verbs such as *achieve, eliminate, identify,* and *schedule.* (See Appendix C for a sample listing of closure verbs.) Activity verbs (such as *understand, ensure, assist, investigate, support, help,* and *champion*) are difficult to measure and to determine completion times and therefore aren't suitable for writing task assignments.

As in the planning phase, each assigned task has a quantity, quality, completion time, and allocated resources aspect to it (the QQTR). Usually, the quantity and time are easy to specify, whereas describing the quality and resources desired are not. Many times, quality is covered through company policy and normal expectations (for example, a selection procedure meeting for the company affirmative action policy or a safety rule conforming to OSHA requirements). Resources can be more difficult to quantify and are usually understood between the manager and the direct report. However, when necessary, they can be specific in terms of available funds, manpower, access to information, and so on. What is important is to have the desired quality and available resources clearly understood.

As will happen from time to time, circumstances will change and a specific task will need to be revised to fit the new situation. In instances where circumstances make it likely that outputs cannot be achieved as specified, or that more could be done, direct reports are accountable to inform the manager in time for adaptive action to be taken. In this way, there will be no surprises. Here, the employee may be able to suggest possible options for the revised task. However, the manager decides what is to be done, including whatever changes are needed in the task assignment.

General Responsibilities

The other type of task assignments are those that fall under the heading "General Responsibilities." These assignments are ongoing in nature. Here are some examples:

- Maintain ongoing monthly contact with key customers.
- Keep abreast of changes in Italian legislation on imports into Italy.
- Keep informed about the marketing strategy of the top two competitors regarding their new products.

Sometimes specific tasks occur as a part of a general responsibility. Using these examples of general responsibilities, specific tasks might be as follows:

- Conduct a two-day annual key customer convention in Chicago in August.
- Obtain translated copies of the new Italian import legislation and present a summary at the marketing meeting in September.
- Submit a report and present findings on the new product launching strategy by our two major competitors at the marketing meeting in May.

For detailed discussions and comparisons of position descriptions and key accountabilities, see Appendices A and B.

Another aspect of writing task assignments is making sure that individual assignments align with the goals of the manager, the manager's manager, and so on up the ladder to the overall goals of the organization (Appendix E, "Making Strategy Work—The Linkage Process," lays out in four steps the entire system of aligning individual accountabilities and task assignments with the overall strategy of the organization).

Linking long-range strategy to individual key accountabilities transforms broad strategic plans into focused operational plans in which all employees understand and feel part of the overall direction and thrust of the organization, both in the short term and the long term.

Action Plan

Now that you have some guidelines as to how best to assign tasks to your team, it is time to consider some action planning. Review the self-assessment you did earlier on task assignment. Research indicates that the "reality" from employee assessments on your managerial leadership practices is about 23 percent lower on average than your self-rating.

Using your newfound skill of writing clear task assignments, prepare some actions on task assignment that you would like to accomplish within the next three months, as suggested by one of the following examples:

- Schedule a meeting in early January with all direct reports to explain the QQTR approach to task assignments.
- By February 1, implement the QQTR format in all task-assignment descriptions.

- Schedule a meeting with each direct report to discuss progress on task assignments and what barriers may be in the way of getting the task done to QQTR. Discuss any possible changes required and options. Meetings are to be completed by April 1.
- By May 1, revise direct reports' previously written task assignments, using closure verbs and specific completion times.
- Review with all direct reports their four to six key general responsibilities and what specific tasks may develop from them during the next six months.

Put on your calendar the preparation dates for your action planning. You have now completed the first critical element of managerial leadership.

What Is Situational Courage?

Before moving on to the second path, let's take a moment to consider the importance of communicating task assignments and their progress—for both the manager and the direct report. Often, these situations require situational courage—the ability for a manager and direct report to speak candidly to each other about work without negative consequences. Here are two scenarios to illustrate this point.

A Tale of Two Meetings

Last year, a training manager, George, was given the assignment to produce six training e-learning modules for the sales staff by the end of this year, an 18-month project. A status review after nine months indicated the project was on target. However, at a meeting just last week with the HR manager, Marie, George revealed that the project had encountered some difficulties and would not be completed as originally scheduled.

Meeting A

George: About the e-module project for sales, we have two completed and ready to go. Another two are close to completion and should be ready by year's end as scheduled. The last two have become a problem. The vendor we have been working with uses Lectora software language for creating the modules and has been doing very good work for us. Unfortunately, they have recently announced bankruptcy and cannot finish the last two modules.

Marie: Why didn't you tell me about this sooner? I just told everyone about the six-module project and planned to introduce it at the annual sales meeting next month. George, I trusted you, and you let me down. Now drop everything you're doing and make this your number-one priority to get back on track.

George: Well, you've been so busy launching the new health insurance plan I didn't want to bother you with this. I actually thought the vendor would complete all six modules, but it turned out not to be possible for them. I'll do my best to work this out.

Summary

The training manager did not have the courage to tell his manager the bad news earlier and was afraid of the possible consequences, hoping somehow he could find a way to complete the last two modules. The blame was put completely on the vendor.

The HR manager was more concerned about her reputation with the sales department than coming up with a satisfactory solution to the problem. She did not have the courage to ask the training manager for possible options and new completion dates. Rather, the discussion focused on completing the project on time as originally planned.

Meeting B

George: About the e-module project for sales, we ran into a bump in the road and two of the six modules will not be ready by year's end as originally scheduled. The vendor is going out of business due to bankruptcy. However, I have an idea that may be better than our original plan.

Marie: Go ahead; I'm listening.

George: We can still announce the launch of the six e-module initiative for the sales function. As you know, three of the six are basic sales principles, fundamental concepts, and company policies and procedures. These three are ready and can go online in January. Call this Phase A, and then Phase B can go online in April. They contain more sophisticated concepts and require more sales experience.

I've contacted the person who has been working on this project for the vendor. She says she would have no problem completing the last modules by April. She's the only one we know who can complete the modules in Lectora. We can pay her from what we salvaged from our vendor's budget and this will probably cost even less because she would be an independent contractor.

This two-phase implementation also allows us to correct any bugs that are found early on so that they can be corrected before Phase B is launched.

Marie: I like the plan. Let's go ahead with it, but keep me informed if you feel I shouldn't announce the two-phase implementation at the upcoming annual sales meeting next month.

George: Thanks. I'm confident it'll work.

Summary

The training manager had the courage to tell his manager that the present plan was not working and to propose a different, possibly better plan. It takes courage to be proactive.

The HR manager had the courage to listen and understand instead of placing blame and focusing on her reputation with the sales function. It takes courage to look for solutions instead of being reactive to a situation.

Action Plan

For the manager:

- Once it has been determined that a problem exists and a serious discussion is required with the direct report, get out from behind your desk and arrange a meeting where the two of you are face-to-face. This supports an adult-to-adult conversation instead of a parent-child one.

- Listen, listen, listen. Try to understand the person's point of view.
- Steer the discussion toward a solution, not just an expanded description of the problem. When appropriate, ask open-ended questions such as, "What are your thoughts on how we can complete this project?"
- When you arrive at a solution, make sure there is joint ownership of the steps to completion.
- Establish periodic (perhaps weekly or monthly) status review sessions to make sure the new plan is working.
- When the program is completed and online, congratulate the direct report for a job well done.

For the direct report:

- Ask for a meeting with the manager. Define the problem clearly.
- Have at least one possible solution to suggest.
- Jointly come to an agreed-upon solution.
- Do your best to make it work.
- Let the manager know if any new problems arise preventing on-time completion.
- Be prepared for follow-up discussions.

4

Path 2: Managerial Meetings

Managers need to have regular, effective, and purposeful meetings with their direct reports for the purpose of problem solving, discussing ideas for solutions, reviewing priorities, and setting context; these and other situational meetings always require two-way communication. Group meetings reduce the tendency for the creation of silos between functions that are subordinate to a single manager, encouraging and enabling cross-functional work flow.

As you did in Path 1, rate yourself (Figure 4-1) on how well you are now conducting your managerial meetings with your direct reports.

Figure 4-1: Self-Assessment for Managerial Meetings

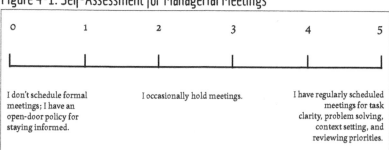

Here is a typical conversation in which one direct report is not aligned with the meeting agenda.

> **Jennifer:** That was a pretty good meeting we just had with our manager. It solved one of my problems I've been having with sales.

> **Matt:** Well, it didn't help me. I wanted to get the team's opinion on an idea I had, but there was no time. Now I'll have to go it alone. By the way, I saw Mike Robbins, the software vendor, coming out of your office yesterday.

> **Jennifer:** That's right; we're looking into a program Mike has that would help us handshake our weekly results into the new SAP system.

> **Matt:** Wow! Mike did something like that for us before you joined the team. It cost over $30,000 and never worked right. Before you go any further with Robbins, I'd be happy to meet with you and walk through the problems we had and perhaps save you some time and budget.

Jennifer: That would be great. I had a feeling something wasn't quite right.

This type of exchange occurs when the manager does not communicate the purpose of the meeting ahead of time, does not distribute an agenda outlining the main focus points, and does not ask for suggestions of items to be included. When this is the case, the meeting becomes a free-for-all with everyone trying to get their "oar in the water." This kind of meeting usually runs overtime and is not very effective. With regular context-setting meetings, the situation described would not have occurred because everyone would have known about the past problems with Mike's vendor and alerted the newcomer to the potential pitfalls.

Content and Process of Meetings

There are two parts to any meeting: the content (the what) and the process (the how). Let's start with the content of managerial meetings and the subjects that could be covered.

There are generally four ways that information has traditionally been shared in organizational meetings: 1) in a unit work review, 2) when generating ideas or problem solving, 3) when communicating news, and 4) individually, in person-to-person meetings.

Unit Work Review Meetings

In the past, the most common meeting was the Monday morning operations meeting—a review of the present status and what needs to get done during the coming week. This was prevalent in such industries as manufacturing and retail. The concept of reviewing unit work as a team still exists, but the frequency and type of the meetings have often changed. Now the focus is on task-assignment progress, clarifying peer and cross-functional issues, and revising timelines. Depending upon the type of work, these kinds of meetings can be scheduled as much as a month apart and can be held through teleconferencing when distances are significant.

Idea Generation and Problem-Solving Meetings

On occasion, there can be a need to have your direct reports (or some of them) join you to help explore possible solutions to a major problem or plan an approach to an upcoming project or issue. This is especially important if these direct reports will be part of the execution of the solution.

Participation leads to Involvement.

Involvement leads to Commitment.

Commitment leads to Motivation.

Brainstorming techniques work well in coming up with new ideas and approaches to a difficult issue. It is important to note that in this type of meeting the manager is seeking information from the direct reports that allows her to make a good decision. Consensus is not the goal here.

Communication Meetings

From time to time, a major event occurs that needs to be communicated down the line. It may be a downsizing of the organization, a closing of a product line, a reduction in the overall budget expenditure, a significant change in the structure and people at the top, a takeover by another organization, or some other situation that could be negatively perceived.

Before false rumors start emerging, it is best that meetings occur throughout the organization to communicate the facts and answer questions as accurately as possible at the time. A written communiqué from the top can also be issued to all concerned on the subject, but that by itself does not replace the personal interaction between a manager and direct reports when a relationship of trust can help maintain employee morale and motivation during periods of organizational crisis. Countless incidents of this nature have been mishandled, resulting in work-time loss, destructive rumors, and, in some instances, loss of valuable talent.

Individual Meetings

Not all meetings need to be group oriented. The manager will often want and need to discuss a task assignment with a direct report. This can occur when a new task is being assigned, the QQTR of an existing task is not on track (for example, the completion time is in jeopardy), or there is a change in the outcome desired.

Now let's look at the process of meetings. It is here where much energy, time, and resources can be saved when certain principles are implemented.

How Many Meetings Are Too Many?

In this organization, meetings had become such an integral part of the culture that no time was available to sit down with another person to discuss an imminent critical issue.

Helen: Hey Joe, I'd like to get together with you to discuss our unit's role in this cross-functional project on the new acquisition. When's a good time?

Joe: I'd love to work with you on this, Helen, but I'm tied up in meetings all week, and Sunday I leave for a plant visit in Mexico. As you know, I'm on six different committees, and they're all meeting for the quarterly reports when I return, which means I don't have any free time until next month. I'm sorry.

Helen: I understand, Joe, but this is important to the smooth integration of our function with the acquisition. Next month will be too late. I guess I'll just go it alone. I'll send you copies of my recommendations. Have a good trip.

A mature team, with good meeting skills, should be able to conclude a productive meeting in one hour or less. What needs to be done to hold an effective meeting? The following list describes some proven techniques used in successful managerial meetings. You can add your own to the list:

- Not all direct reports need to be at all meetings. Be selective and let nonattendees get on with their work. Put them on the list to receive a summary of the meeting so they don't think they are missing out.
- Send out a brief agenda so that people can get organized and bring the proper data to the meeting. State what kind of meeting it will be (work status, context setting, problem solving, and so forth). Include the starting and finishing times in the agenda.

- Stick to the timeframe. Start on time whether or not everyone has arrived. They will soon learn you mean what you say regarding the start time. Besides, it is wasteful for the rest of the team to wait for one or two stragglers, and it extends the overall time of the meeting.
- Finish on time even though everything hasn't been accomplished. Everyone will quickly adjust to this and work toward completion in subsequent meetings.

Time Management

At a large company headquartered in New York City, a top-level meeting had been going on without any sign of closure. It was 5 p.m., and one of the vice presidents got up and started to leave the room:

> **President**: Where are you going, Jennifer? We're not finished yet.

> **Vice president**: John, we've been at this for three hours with no conclusions. I've got a train to catch so I'll be home with my family by dinnertime. There is nothing more I can add at this time.

This exchange broke up the meeting. The president was quite disturbed at the time but admitted later that he learned something.

- Designate someone in the room as the timekeeper, letting the team know that "we are 30 minutes into the meeting and have only covered the first item on the agenda," or "there are only 10 minutes left and we should begin to summarize our conclusions."
- Have a computer projector, flipchart, or whiteboard in the room so that everyone sees the same data (options, conclusions,

or next steps). Without this, people leave with their own notes, which are certain not to be the same. The manager can designate someone in the room to be the scribe.

- If possible, have a clock on the wall for all to see.
- Start a meeting at 11 a.m. or 4 p.m. It's amazing how quickly things get done.
- Discourage (or even eliminate) the use of personal electronics during the meeting.
- Before deciding to have a meeting, think about whether or not a teleconference could accomplish the same thing. Sometimes, a short teleconference prior to a meeting can save time at the meeting (data to bring, who will make a brief presentation on what, meeting results expected, and so forth).
- If at all possible, a meeting summary by the manager should go out to all direct reports indicating what was accomplished, what was not accomplished, and action agreed upon, including the date, time, and location of a follow-up meeting if one is necessary. This step may appear redundant, but it is also a learning device, and future team meetings will benefit from "closing the loop."
- About halfway through the meeting, "suspend business" for two minutes and declare a "time-out" to discuss how the process is working. Are we on track or off on a tangent? Is everyone participating as expected? Will we finish on time? Should we save one topic for another time? This brief interlude helps to focus the group back on the purpose of the meeting and the agenda.
- There are times when it is worthwhile to combine two types of meetings within one session for efficiency. This works well

provided that the two are clearly identified and separated. For example, it may be beneficial to have a problem-solving meeting followed by a context-setting meeting (or vice versa) all within two hours. A break between the two helps to change the mindset.

- Keep members aware of the cost of meetings. I once had a small machine that, by inputting the salaries of people at a meeting, would operate like a taxi meter, providing the ongoing meeting cost. When people saw the thousands of dollars accumulating, it made a definite impact on the length of the meeting. Today, this can easily be done using a bit of software and then projecting the cost on a screen. Meetings cost money. Long meetings waste money.

Reducing 30 minutes per meeting throughout the organization yields a great deal of resource savings over the course of a year. It is impressive to do the calculations. As the 18th-century statesman Lord Chesterfield wrote, "Take care of the minutes, and the hours will take care of themselves." But it is more than that. Research shows that as meetings become more time effective they yield better results and stimulate valuable participation by direct reports. By applying the suggestions in this chapter, a manager is in a better position to make final decisions. Henry David Thoreau once wrote, "It is not enough to be busy—so are the ants—the question is what we are busy about."

At a convenient time after a meeting, review what you wanted to accomplish and what you actually got done in terms of both the content and the process. Review the before, during, and after planning suggestions here in the checklist. Meeting improvement is an ongoing process. Make plans to do better next time.

Managerial Meetings Checklist

Successful managers:

- ☑ Meet regularly with their team of immediate reports.
- ☑ Seek input from their direct reports during these meetings.
- ☑ Make decisions using information obtained at meetings.
- ☑ Don't seek consensus, but make decisions that direct reports agree they can implement.
- ☑ Prepare the meeting agenda, keep the meeting focused, and ensure follow-up tasks are assigned and completed.

Action Plan

Now it is time to do some action planning for improved performance regarding managerial meetings. Given what you now know, write out some of the things that you plan to do for meetings during the next few months. Here are some examples:

Before my next meeting with my direct reports, I will:

- Decide who should attend.
- Send out an agenda ahead of time.
- State what type of meeting it is.
- Show starting and finishing times.

During my next meeting with my direct reports, I will:

- Use a flipchart or whiteboard for clarity.
- Get everyone involved.
- Start on time and stay on time.
- Discourage use of cell phones or email.

After my next meeting with my direct reports, I will:

- Send out a summary of what was accomplished, and what was not.

- Ask for feedback as to what can be done to improve meetings.
- If possible, set up the date, time, type, purpose, and agenda for the next meeting.
- Ask for possible items to be included in the next meeting.

5

Path 3: Context Setting

Managers are accountable for setting context for all their direct reports on a regular basis. It is important that these employees see how their work fits into the bigger picture—their manager's job and the organization as a whole. It is also important that they see how their work fits with the work of their peers and colleagues.

Rate yourself (Figure 5-1) on how you feel you are setting context with your direct reports:

Figure 5-1: Self-Assessment: Context Setting

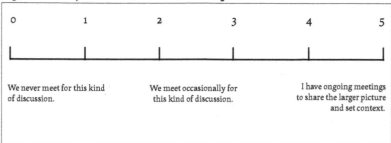

| 0 | 1 | 2 | 3 | 4 | 5 |

We never meet for this kind of discussion.

We meet occasionally for this kind of discussion.

I have ongoing meetings to share the larger picture and set context.

Managers need to share background information on an ongoing basis so that direct reports can make informed decisions and collaborate with their peers and colleagues without having to go back to the manager. Setting clear context for direct reports improves their ability to accomplish their task assignments in relation to the rest of the unit's work. It saves time for the manager and for these employees as well.

There are three types of information sharing. Direct reports need to:

1. Know about the manager's goals and issues so that they can see how their individual work output fits into the unit's work output.

2. Possess the bigger picture so they understand relevant issues being dealt with by the organization as a whole.

3. Know about one another's task assignments, enabling them to work knowledgeably together to reduce the silo effect.

Paying Attention to the Bigger Picture

Here is an example of a context-setting meeting in which Julia, the unit manager, is setting the context for her team on all three types of information sharing:

Julia: As you'll recall from my email outlining our meeting agenda, I've put aside time to talk about our unit goals and my issues and concerns in reaching them. It helps when we all see what we're striving for as a unit and how each of you contributes to the total output. Related to this, I've learned this morning that we continue to be over budget on the new high-speed copier production line. I've been reminded that this new line is supposed to contribute significantly to the corporate profit numbers for next year, so we'll have to get our costs down. Hank, what's going on in inventory control?

Hank: Well, Julia, we've been concentrating on getting the material inventory down for that new line, and it seems to be working. Right now, it's about half of what it was when the line was first launched. This is good for us as we don't have a large supply of parts on our books, especially since George tells me there may be some part modifications coming up. And, of course, it gives us more space. We've also developed relationships with some good backup suppliers in the event one or more of our primary ones have trouble delivering on time or their quality drops below our specifications. I'm not sure how much further inventory reduction we should make at this time as production of this copier has been very erratic. Last month, it was shut down for a while. Now I understand there's talk of a second shift because of a surge in demand.

Julia: Thanks, Hank. It looks as though you'll have to stay in constant touch with George until this gets worked out. As you point out, keeping the material inventory as low as possible saves a significant amount of money for the company. Now, let's hear from George.

George: I'd like to keep discussing the new copier line if I may, Julia. The other assembly lines are mature and running well. Hank and I have been talking about getting the inventory levels down on the mature lines. This should not be a problem as the demand is steady and predictable. For some reason, orders for this new copier coming from sales are all over the place. At times, we can't keep up, and at other times, there is nothing. We do some stockpiling of subassemblies and finished machines. However, with requests for customizing and our continuous modifications, too much stockpiling is a losing proposition. When large orders come in and delivery time is short, we may have to go to a second shift. This needs to be compared to using overtime for the employees on the regular line. Right now, we're doing a little of this and a little of that to get the deliveries out the door on time. I've talked with Chris, the master scheduler, and he has no idea how to smooth out the demand at this time.

Julia: OK, George. Let's hope that the demand evens out soon, and as the line matures, we can make an intelligent decision whether to go with a second shift or not. Let's you and I meet next week with Chris and see if we can improve the situation.

Tom, our contracts with the three trucking companies will be up for renewal in two months, and I'd like your input into what changes should be made in the contracts.

Tom: Julia, listening to Hank and George helps me to understand why our shipping has become so unpredictable. Incidentally, our contracts with the three trucking lines we use do not include any clauses for special shipments, such as overnight delivery, and they have been charging us high premiums for this. It makes sense from their point of view as they have to locate an extra vehicle and driver on short notice. If this keeps up, we may want to have our own delivery system for these special circumstances, but this gets us back in the trucking business, which we dropped a few years ago.

Julia: You're right, Tom. George may have some ideas before we talk to the trucking firms. Check with him in two weeks to see where all this stands. Then you and I should meet about the contracts.

You may have heard that next Thursday there will be a board of directors meeting here. There's been a request for them to visit the copier machines assembly floor and the ATM assembly area in the afternoon. So if you see some people all dressed up walking around your areas, just smile and answer any questions they may have. Make sure you have extra safety glasses handy.

Context meetings of this type inform each direct report of issues and concerns of the manager, senior management, and the other employees. On occasion, the manager's manager attends the meeting, which is beneficial in two ways: in this example, she describes some of the major issues confronting the department, function, or business unit and learns about the problems and challenges facing management at the lower levels. Context setting can be carried out as part of regular managerial meetings or a special meeting for this purpose.

There are times when context setting is appropriate between the manager and only one of the direct reports. Here, the manager provides context for this employee by showing how the completion of his tasks fits with the other work that is being done in the unit and by describing the larger outcome the manager is seeking for the total unit.

Context-Setting Checklist

Successful managers:

- ☑ Set context for their employees on a regular basis.
- ☑ Provide the larger picture within which they are working.
- ☑ Let direct reports know about issues and concerns of the manager.
- ☑ Enable direct reports to know about one another's work.
- ☑ Reduce the silo effect within the unit and between units.

Action Plan

List some action plans you would like to implement. Here are some examples:

- As a start, schedule a meeting specifically for context setting, inviting your manager to attend.

- Lay out the guidelines and agenda for this meeting in advance.
- Once initiated, set aside part of your regular meetings for context setting.
- Get feedback from the team regarding the benefit of this activity and invite suggestions.

6

Path 4: Feedback

It may be the most unanswered question in organizations today: "How am I doing?" This can be interpreted as a lack of feedback on the effort individuals invest in their work and the results achieved. Everyone has an idea as to how they are doing (sometimes a bit self-exaggerated), but feedback from a key person, such as the individual's immediate manager, gives the person a unique look at a different reality. It's always important to hear it from the boss. After all, your manager has some control over your progress with the company, including your present and future compensation.

Positive recognition is one of the four factors involved in employee motivation. The other three are achievement, growth, and responsibility. Timely, positive feedback, when deserved, is a simple way of letting employees know they are important and that they count. It helps build a healthy self-image. It is important to remember that the average workers spend more than 50 percent of their waking hours on the job during the work week.

Giving Positive and Constructive Feedback

Does this sound familiar?

Courtney: Hi Susan . . . how did your meeting with Julia go?

Susan: Good, I guess. We agreed on a new timeline for next year's budget proposal and an interview deadline for George's replacement. Not very exciting stuff! However, I took the opportunity to ask her how she thought I've been doing since I've been in the job more than six months now.

Courtney: That's very courageous of you! What did she say?

Susan: I think it caught her by surprise. She didn't say anything for a while, and then said I was doing OK, and that there were a few things I need to learn to become fully functional. I already knew that.

Courtney: Did you get the answer you were looking for?

Susan: Not really. "Doing OK" doesn't do much for me. I would like to hear from my manager some specifics of where I am doing well, in addition to where I need to improve and how to go about it.

Courtney: Well, don't expect too much from her on that score. She's not that kind of person.

Direct reports need to know what they are doing well and where they need to improve. It is the manager's responsibility to let them know on a regular basis how they are performing. Depending upon the situation, feedback can be positive, or it can be corrective. Feedback should be frequent, accurate, specific, and timely (FAST).

As we have been doing with the other subjects, rate yourself on how well you believe you are doing in giving feedback to your direct reports (Figure 6-1).

Figure 6-1: Self-Assessment Feedback

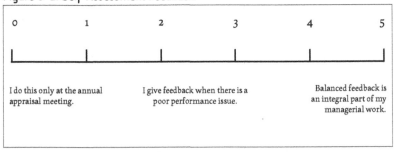

Telling someone "you're doing a great job" is not going to have the impact that specific praise, detailed and relevant, could have. Develop a list of "openers" that you can use to keep your praise specific. Here are several to get you started; then try writing a few of your own.

1. "You really made a difference by____."
2. "I'm impressed with____. What are the next steps?"
3. "You got my attention with____. How can we follow up on this?"
4. "You're doing top-quality work on____."

5. "You're right on the mark with____."
6. "One of the things I enjoy most about you is____. It's becoming contagious in the unit."
7. "You can be proud of yourself for____."
8. "We couldn't have done it without your____. I really appreciate it."
9. "What an effective way to____. How can we use it elsewhere?"
10. "You've made my day because of____."

When the opportunity arises, give some positive feedback to a direct report in a meeting where the person's peers are present. This multiplies the impact many times and will be remembered by everyone. There will also be times when a group, team, or task force should be recognized for an extraordinary accomplishment. Select the proper moment for this to happen. Remember the old saying: "Praise in public, criticize in private."

Feedback Reminders

For some managers, giving praise and constructive feedback comes naturally, and they enjoy this aspect of their interpersonal relationships. Many, however, need to develop the feedback habit. This is where feedback reminders come in handy. Here are two real-life examples from my professional experience in which habits were successfully developed using devices and techniques to support desired behavior.

A Fish Called Feedback

John was in his mid-40s. As a production engineer, he worked his way up the ladder and became general manager of the company's largest plant, which employed more than 4,000 people. Things were going very well for him.

One day, John decided that his managers and supervisors (about 200) should get some feedback on how well they were performing their various managerial responsibilities and that this feedback should primarily come from their direct reports and those directly under them. John also participated in the assessment.

The assessment went well, and the responses helped formulate a series of workshops on the subjects needing improvement. But one thing happened that surprised John. His own ratings came in high, averaging 4.2 on a scale of 0 to 5 (where 5 is ideal), except for one factor—feedback. When he examined all the data, he didn't want to talk about his feedback score. A few weeks later, we spoke on the phone and the conversation went like this:

John: Before we hang up, Doctor Fred, I want to tell you what I did about my low feedback score on the assessment. At first, it was hard to swallow as I believe in both positive and constructive feedback, and I think I know how to give it. I came to the conclusion that with everything going on here—the expansion and all—I got into the bad habit of concentrating only on minute-to-minute and hour-to-hour things, ignoring one of the ongoing managerial practices critical to the culture at the plant.

Fred: That sounds like the correct diagnosis, John. What do you plan to do about it? As you know, the best way to break a bad habit is with a new habit.

John: I've already done it. I bought a goldfish and bowl and put it on my desk. I call the fish Feedback, and it is the first thing I see in the morning when I come to work. Since the fish swims around, it is a constant reminder and gets my attention. It may seem like a stupid idea, but it works for me. I've improved my old behavior with a new approach. This fish is my reminder.

5 Coins

Phil is a CEO who is very good at giving negative feedback. In fact, he enjoys it. He would like to be more balanced; however, new habits are difficult to acquire without some help.

Fred: Phil, I'd like you to try something that may seem silly at first, but it may work. Take five coins (silver dollars are good), and when you dress in the morning, put all five in your left-front pants pocket. They will feel a bit awkward, but this is your reminder. During the work day, every time you give positive feedback, move one of the coins to the right-front pants pocket. Try it. It's a simple way to begin a new habit.

About a month later, I called Phil to check in.

Fred: Hi Phil, how's your positive feedback habit coming along?

Phil: I'm glad you called. I tried your somewhat bizarre idea, and for the first week, all the coins ended up where they started, in my left pocket. Then I started to move a few, and in two weeks, all five ended up in my right pocket. I stopped using the coins.

Fred: That's great. Do you think you'll keep it up?

Phil: Absolutely because I see both the reaction in the people and my reaction to their reaction. It has been a real eye-opener for me. Incidentally, it evens works at home with my family. Thanks again.

Negative or Constructive? Understanding the Difference

There are times when constructive feedback is appropriate. Some people call this negative feedback, corrective feedback, or constructive criticism. It starts early in life from teachers, parents, and older siblings saying such things as "Stop that!" "Don't do that!" "Do this!" All this feedback is based on a parent-child relationship. Over time, as we receive negative feedback, we also learn how to give it. As a manager, we become the parent and the employee the child. Constructive feedback works best using an adult-to-adult approach. When giving constructive feedback, focus on what the desired results should have been and not as much on how to do it. Adults learn best not by being told what to do or what not to do, but by experiencing the consequences of their actions (more on this in chapter 8, "Path 6: Coaching Direct Reports").

Giving Feedback Checklist

Successful managers:

- ☑ Include feedback in their managerial leadership practices. Timely, positive feedback is underrated and underused by most managers.
- ☑ Keep feedback balanced. Many managers tend only to give negative feedback and find it difficult to give praise. Positive and constructive feedback can go together. Remember, when you point a finger at someone, three fingers are pointing back at you.
- ☑ Create a reminder device. As with the fish called Feedback, create a device to remind yourself that people want and need feedback about their performance. This could be a symbol on your mirror, telephone, or computer. It could be an object on your desk.
- ☑ Give regular feedback. At a minimum, personal effectiveness feedback should take place every time a direct report completes a task as given, or lets the manager know he may not be able to complete the task to specified QQTR.
- ☑ Keep the discussion on an adult-to-adult basis, not parent-to-child.
- ☑ Make feedback FAST.

Action Plan

List some possible actions you can take to increase your positive feedback to direct reports and improve your approach to constructive feedback. Here are some examples:

- Create a positive feedback reminder that you see every morning.
- Extend this concept to the evenings and weekends with your family.
- To make positive feedback a habit, keep a temporary log of your progress in giving positive feedback to your direct reports.
- Plan your constructive feedback prior to the discussion with the employee.

Focus on the mutually agreed-upon results to be obtained, allowing the employee to suggest revisions in procedures.

7

Path 5: Performance Appraisal

A personal effectiveness appraisal needs to take place every time a direct report completes a key task or brings a problem of a task assignment for reconsideration. This discussion provides an ongoing appraisal of the employee's personal effectiveness. The manager's collection of significant events of this kind is the basis for the manager's periodic informal reviews. At a minimum, each direct report should have a midyear and annual review.

The formal annual appraisal meeting acts as a summary of the feedback and coaching meetings that have been held throughout the year. It is part of an ongoing process and should contain few, if any, surprises.

As you have done on previous subjects, rate yourself on how you presently use the annual appraisal meeting (Figure 7-1).

Figure 7-1: Performance Appraisal Self-Assessment

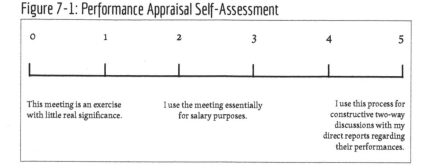

Informal and Formal Appraisals

Has something like this ever happened to you?

Jack: Hey George, thanks for having lunch with me today. I had my annual appraisal meeting this morning, and it went on for two and a half hours. It was a tough time. I knew it was coming, so I prepared for it. I put together notes on the things the boss helped me through and also some of the things I did very well on my own.

George: Wow, that sounds rough, Jack, but did he appreciate your approach?

Jack: Not really. He asked me what I thought my overall rating should be, which I told him, and he responded that it was too high. He then spent the rest of the morning defending his rating, and I gave him specific examples supporting my self-rating.

George: How did it end up?

Jack: I don't know. He said he would need more time to think about it.

Appraising a direct report should not be a once-a-year exercise, but rather an accumulation of mini appraisals that happen throughout the year when an assignment has been completed or revised. Most of these will be verbal discussions. Some managers like the idea of keeping a special folder (called a performance folder) for each direct report where notes (good and not so good) on the individual's performance are accumulated and referred to at the informal midyear review. Action plans can be established for the second half of the year and the process continues.

By year's end, there are sufficient data to compile a summary of ongoing mini appraisals resulting in an overall annual appraisal. Using this method ensures there will be no surprises for the direct report because significant accomplishments or incidents have been previously discussed and documented. As a Chinese proverb attests, "The faintest ink is stronger than the fondest memory."

The manager's collection of significant events of how well a direct report met the expectations of the key accountabilities of the role is the basis for the manager's periodic reviews and annual summary of personal effectiveness. This information becomes the foundation for the manager's judgment of an employee's overall effectiveness.

Checklist for Performance Appraisal

Successful managers:

☑ Understand that this is not a once-a-year exercise. It is an accumulation of mini appraisals that occur throughout the year.

☑ Keep a performance folder on each direct report and include any notes, comments, and discussions that have occurred with the employee throughout the year. This should include both positive and negative issues. This gives the annual appraisal meeting a foundation of specific incidents and helps to focus on objective data instead of personal opinions.

☑ Give direct reports ample notice before the annual appraisal meeting date and encourage them to prepare for the meeting.

☑ Allow direct reports sufficient time to express their views on their effectiveness during the meeting. Listen actively to what they have to say and let them know their concerns have been heard.

☑ Separate salary issues from the performance appraisal meeting. The meeting should be on the individual's past performance and potential future growth in the role. Discussing salary issues at this time changes the focus to one of monetary concerns and away from performance.

☑ Plan and do a midyear appraisal. This helps bring the direct report up to date on any performance issues that need improvement and any task assignments that need revision. Waiting for a once-a-year annual appraisal is less effective and not recommended.

☑ Plan how the formal meeting will happen. Focus on two things: the accomplishment of the tasks assigned to the role and the development of the individual in the role.

☑ Have the formal meeting in a neutral setting, not across the desk in a manager-employee positioning. Hold all phone calls and make sure there are no other interruptions. Give the employee the opportunity to feel equal in terms of communicating facts, opinions, and feelings.

Keep in mind that there are subtle distortions that could distract from a proper appraisal, such as:

- a tendency to judge overall effectiveness based on the employee's most recent behavior
- judging all employees at or near average
- giving only above-average ratings to avoid confrontation.

Action Plan

List some actions you can take to improve the informal and formal performance appraisal of your direct reports. Here are some examples:

- Create a performance folder for each direct report and add written notes and comments, both positive and negative, throughout the year.
- Do a midyear appraisal, giving the individual insight as to your judgment to date and helping set plans for the remainder of the year.
- Give the direct report ample time to prepare for the formal annual appraisal.
- During these discussions, allow individuals sufficient time to express their viewpoints and actively listen to them.

8

Path 6: Coaching Direct Reports

Skilled coaching is one of the critical paths to effective managerial leadership. It is not to be confused with training, mentoring, counseling, or teaching (see Glossary). Each has its place, but the focus of managerial coaching is to:

- Help the individual acquire any additional needed skills in the role.
- Identify areas needing improvement for performing effectively in the role.
- Help the person understand the full range of his role.

Managerial coaching is an interactive process between the manager and her direct reports, targeted toward the performance improvement of the individual in the role. When a manager takes on the role of coach, she needs to keep four things in mind:

1. The manager is in a power position, which can affect the dynamics of the situation.
2. The issue in question should be specific, not general in nature.
3. The manager has responsibilities to the organization in relation to the individual's performance.
4. The manager should believe that the person values the work in the role and wants to improve.

Rate yourself on how you think you are doing as a coach to your direct reports (Figure 8-1):

Figure 8-1: Coaching Self-Assessment

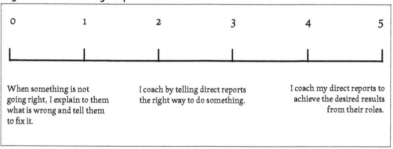

Coaching Growth Within the Role

Managers are accountable to be proactive coaches, helping direct reports to understand the full range of their roles and what they need to do to perform the work of that role effectively. Managers coach direct reports using adult-learning principles. Adults learn not by being told but by experiencing the consequences of their actions.

Helen: Good morning, George. I'm looking forward to your report so I can discuss it at the senior management meeting this afternoon.

George: Well, I'm sorry, Helen, but it won't be ready until next week—something beyond my control.

Helen: Why? What happened? This isn't good.

George: Well, everything was working fine. The data were coming in on time, and I left a week for Tim to pull it all together, but he came down with the flu and is not due back until next week.

Helen: My manager won't be happy. George, what could we have done to prevent this from happening?

George: Well, I made what I thought was a sound assumption that Tim would have ample time to pull all this together. It never entered my mind that he wouldn't be available.

Helen: George, let me ask you again. You had an important task assignment with a specific completion date. What went wrong?

George: I made an assumption that turned out to be wrong.

Helen: What can you do in the future to not have this happen again?

George: This has never happened to me before. I learned an important lesson—always have a contingency plan, a plan B, when you make a key assumption. For example, I could have had Shirley shadow this project enough for her to take over in an emergency. It would also have given her a development opportunity, which she would have liked. I can assure you this will never happen again.

Helen: George, it's good that you learned something from this incident. However, you still dropped the ball by not letting me know in time for you and me to do something about it right away. Is that a fair conclusion?

George: Yes, I guess so. I didn't realize how important this was. And I made a mistake not keeping you informed of the situation as soon as I realized there was a potential problem. That's the second lesson I learned. It won't happen again.

In this incident the manager was able to coach the direct report into an improved behavior in real time. Note that the manager was not telling the person what to do differently but allowing the individual to state what went wrong and describe acceptable future behavior.

This is an example in which the problem was clear, and the direct report was motivated to do better next time. Many times, managerial coaching can be accomplished through a simple process of allowing the person to analyze what went wrong and plan future improvement, such as what was done here. However, there are times when the issues are larger in scope and will take more time and effort to resolve.

A 5-Step Process for Managerial Coaching

Here is a process that can be used as a guideline for most managerial coaching situations.

Step 1: State Purpose of Meeting

When meeting with a direct report, be clear about the purpose of the discussion. Describe the situation as you have observed it. Use specific incidents and facts to support your case. Define the desired outcomes and the expectations you would like to see as a result of this discussion.

Step 2: Listen to Direct Report

Give the individual the opportunity to respond. Try to get agreement on the facts. Listen carefully.

When the person is finished explaining the situation from his viewpoint, use open-ended questions to approach mutual understanding of the issue. For example, "What do you think is the problem here?" or "What do you think are the results we should be expecting?"

It is important for the manager and the individual being coached to come to agreement on what the problem or issue is and that something needs to be to solve it. Without this agreement, any solution will be marginal at best.

Step 3: Get Problem Agreement

Before identifying solutions, it is critical that the person being coached understands and agrees with the desired outcomes as covered in Step 2. A collaborative approach can then be used to explore possible actions.

It is very tempting to tell the individual what she should do. However, before the manager offers a solution, the employee should be asked to suggest ways to handle the situation and achieve the expected perfomance. Many times, this person is the best resource for insight and problem solving, especially in developing ideas for overcoming barriers to improved performance. Here again, good use of open-ended questions will move the discussion in the desired direction and give the individual joint ownership of the final action plan. For example, "How would you go about solving this problem?" or "What are some ways we can reach our goal?"

As the discussion continues, a number of options for a solution will evolve, some from the individual and some from the manager.

Step 4: Establish a Joint Action Plan

It is now time to put together an agreed-upon action plan. To be effective, it is essential for the direct report to be an active participant in this process. Having the individual suggest next steps and a timeline is helpful. It is also a good idea for the manager to ask how he can help in accomplishing the action plan. A review of the final plan should be done by the manager at this time.

Before making the assumption that the problem is resolved, the manager should ask the person being coached to summarize what was accomplished in the meeting, especially the detailed action plan agreed upon (with next steps and a timeline). This ensures that the manager and the individual have the same understanding of what is to happen. Any discrepancies in the understanding of the agreed-upon action plan are handled at this time. Notes should be taken by both individuals.

Step 5: Follow-Up

The manager then sets one or more follow-up dates to review progress. Supportive feedback during the follow-up meeting in the form of positive comments and suggestions to the direct report would be appropriate. Praise is a powerful motivator. If sufficient progress is not apparent, the manager would need to review with the person the reasons why and jointly revise the action plan as appropriate.

Putting the 5 Steps Into Action

The following example illustrates the five-step managerial coaching process in action:

> **Tina:** Good morning, Tony. Please sit down. We need to visit for a few minutes. I was talking to Sara in accounting last Monday. She mentioned that she's not getting the data from us that she needs every Friday, and it's causing her people to have to submit a revised report when she does receive the data. As you know, as manager of compensation and benefits, one of your important assignments this year is to meet with the accounting folks and develop a streamlined process to deliver in a timely way what they need and what the new SAP system requires. How is that coming along?

> **Tony:** I know, Tina. The completion date on that is the end of this month, but there's no way I can get it done by then. I was meaning to talk to you about this.

Tina: I was looking over your key accountabilities for the year, Tony, and it seems that you're running behind on a number of them. Am I correct?

Tony: Well, yes, that's right, but I'm hoping to catch up in the next few months. I've been working late most days, but there doesn't seem to be enough time to do everthing.

Tina: Tony, you are a very hard and loyal worker, and I'm glad you're on our team. However, I really want to see you get caught up on your key accountabilities. What do you think is the problem?

Tony: As I see it, Tina, it's a time problem. On my whiteboard each morning when I arrive, I list the things I need to do to work on my key tasks, the ones that were established at the beginning of the year. I have no problem scoping these out and planning to get them done. However, as you know, I am the spokesperson for our area on cross-functional issues. Even problems within our function are directed to me to discuss and help resolve. These are usually one-on-one discussions with another person. With the rapid expansion of the organization, more and more of these critical discussions are being scheduled. I must admit, I've got a talent for problem solving and have the required interpersonal skills, so I enjoy doing this kind of work very much. Sometimes, the discussions go beyond the initial subject, but I like helping people with their problems. I only schedule these meetings in the morning so I can get other things done in the afternoon. Each meeting takes about an hour, so only three can be scheduled for any given day. Sometimes I do one over lunch. My present backlog is more than two weeks long.

On top of this, I have another project I'm working on that takes at least five hours per week. This is the continual improvement project that I suggested at our last team meeting and you assigned to me. It's a significant project, and I'm happy to be the lead person on it. It'll save us a good deal of time and resources when it becomes operational, which I would estimate is in about six months. When successfully implemented, the concept can be exported to other parts of the organization for additional savings.

It's these two important ongoing activities that are interfering with my staying on top of the other assignments you've given me.

Tina: You've described the situation very well, Tony. I certainly hadn't looked at it this way. As you said, it seems to be a time problem. I would suggest it may also be a priority issue. Let's examine what you can do differently without staying late every evening.

Tony: Agreed, and I'll need your help in setting priorities. I'd like to start with the problem-solving sessions that are taking up half of my time every day. In the beginning, I could fit the discussions in, but now they've grown in number and duration. Of course, we could train someone else to share this load, like John, for example, but this would take more time up front. Everyone who could do this type of work already has a full workload.

Tina: Tony, you said that you really enjoy helping other people with their work problems as they interface with our function. You also said that sometimes the discussions drift away to other subjects that need attention and, if solved, would help the organization as a whole. Is that correct?

Tony: Yes, that's true. I look forward to helping other people, and they seem to be very appreciative. However, I've got to do something about this, because it's definitely interfering with my other key assignments.

Tina: What could you do to reduce the time spent on these discussions by half—90 minutes instead of three hours? That's 30 minutes per person instead of 60 minutes.

Tony: Well, I could schedule only Tuesdays and Thursdays for these meetings, but that would create a huge backlog. I could schedule only two per morning instead of three but again, that would result in a constant backlog. I wonder if I could accomplish the main thrust of the session in 30 minutes instead of 60 minutes. It would mean staying on target, working from a structured approach, and only confronting the immediate situation without trying to solve all the other side issues. It would also mean keeping a three-per-day schedule with little or no backlog.

Tina: I like your idea of a more structured format. You may find that this approach will work for you. It's certainly worth a try. If you can develop a one-page form, a template that the individual completes before the meeting, which follows a sound decision-making sequence, it will save a good deal of time. It will enable the individual to think about problem definition, barriers, goals, and options before meeting with you. Completion of the form will also give the person insight into how to solve the problem without coming to you to solve it for them. What do you think?

Tony: I like it, Tina. I'll start on this right away. The other subject I mentioned was the continual improvement project that I'm heading; it takes at least five hours of my time each week.

Tina: How's that coming along, Tony?

Tony: Slowly, but we're making some headway. Paul is doing the heavy lifting right now. He's a great help.

Tina: Tony, it's important that you get caught up on your key assignments. What do you think of having Paul take over the project for the rest of the year with your involvement being only one of coaching him from time to time?

Tony: Well, I really like managing the project, but it makes sense to put Paul in charge right now. It'll free up valuable time for me. Between that and the change in my cross-functional problem-solving meetings, I should have no problem getting my regular work done. Thanks for your help, Tina.

Tina: Great! Let's get together in a month to see how things are going. Put a meeting on the schedule at a time that works for both of us.

This example illustrates how the employee, over time, had allowed work preferences to interfere with his role accountabilities and needed some coaching before the situation deteriorated further. Also, the manager, in delegating the continual improvement project to him, did not factor in the additional time required. For both Tina and Tony, this coaching meeting was successful.

As stated in the beginning of this chapter, coaching is one of the most critical skills required of managers. It takes time and a commitment to help others in developing within their present roles. (This is not to be confused with developing people for future roles. This is best done by the manager's manager.)

The coaching relationship is collaborative between the manager and the direct report. It can best be described as, "How can we solve the problem?" It involves jointly identifying the performance problem, agreeing upon goals to achieve improvement, and determining specific action plans with timelines.

Checklist for Managerial Coaching

Successful managers:

- ☑ Initiate the coaching process in a timely manner and when they think the direct report is ready to participate.
- ☑ Select a location for the meeting that will be free of interruptions.
- ☑ Are descriptive, not evaluative, by describing actual behavior, not judgments on the behavior. This helps avoid putting the person on the defensive.
- ☑ Ask open-ended questions in which a yes or no reply can't be given.
- ☑ Listen attentively. You cannot talk and listen at the same time. A good ratio would be 70 percent listening and 30 percent talking.
- ☑ Paraphrase the person's responses for clarity and mutual understanding.
- ☑ Keep the focus on the performance problem and solution, not on the individual.
- ☑ Ask the person being coached to summarize the discussion at the end of the meeting, including next steps and timelines.
- ☑ Take into account both the individual's needs and the organization's needs, resulting in a win-win situation.

Action Plan

Here are some ways you can improve your managerial coaching effort:

- By (date), decide what coaching sessions you should conduct within the next three months.

- Before your next managerial coaching session, review the five-step process described in this chapter and plan the discussion.
- Prior to a coaching session, prepare your opening statement, which will put the individual at ease and, at the same time, clearly state the purpose of the meeting.
- Develop skill in using open-ended questions in which a yes or no answer can't be given.
- Practice paraphrasing an individual's remarks so that you will be able to do this easily during a coaching session.

9

Path 7: Continual Improvement

As with the preceding paths, continual improvement (CI) is integrated into the manager's role. Improving the unit's processes, systems, and procedures is an ongoing managerial leadership practice and, like the others, becomes a habit that will lead to a higher level of performance for the entire unit.

There are four steps necessary to have a successful CI effort in an organization (Lee 2007):

1. Hold managers accountable for the process.
2. Maintain an ongoing analysis.
3. Review and prioritize improvement projects and assign as tasks.
4. Provide assistance from staff specialists.

Improvement in a process, system, or procedure is seldom an accident or a normal progression of events. It is almost always the result of a conscious effort of one or more people to upgrade an activity so that it can be done more efficiently or produce better results. This can mean less time involved, less manpower used, higher quality, or increased quantity and, of course, reduction in costs.

Developing a plan to embed continual improvement into a manager's ongoing activities may not seem as pertinent as the other six paths. The primary reason for this is that, given the manager's busy minute-to-minute schedule and overall workload, improvement in general has no specific completion date; it can be put off, postponed for a rainy day. "If it isn't broken, don't fix it" can become the operational attitude. However, the best time to improve things is while they are still functioning, before they become ineffective.

On the scale shown, rate yourself on how well you think you are doing on this important managerial leadership practice (Figure 9-1):

Figure 9-1: Self-Assessment: Context Setting

0	1	2	3	4	5

No improvement projects of this kind have been initiated in recent years.	Occasionally an improvement project is assigned when it becomes urgent.	Process improvement is ongoing with at least one project active at all times.

Improving Processes, Systems, and Procedures

Continual improvement of work processes is the responsibility of each manager. Managers prioritize a list of improvement projects and share this list with their manager and direct reports. It is reviewed on a regular basis. At any time, there will be at least one improvement project assigned as a task to an individual in the unit or to an ad hoc team.

Two phases are suggested in a CI effort, one ongoing and one specific:

Phase 1: Ongoing

Create an environment where direct reports openly offer suggestions for improvement at any time. This allows for spontaneity. The manager maintains a list of these suggestions and adds her own.

The manager needs to refrain from saying to a direct report, "That's a good idea. Send me a report on this with all the details—why, how, who, time, and cost/benefit analysis." This approach to a suggestion seldom goes anywhere and becomes a burden rather than an opportunity. It will be interpreted as extra work and will inhibit future suggestions.

Phase 2: Specific

Set aside all or part of a managerial meeting to identify possible improvement projects. It is important for the manager to involve direct reports in the identification and subsequent development of improvement projects. They will have some good ideas, and there will be synergy. In addition, their involvement now will help later in the implementation stage.

Here are seven steps that will help in launching a continual improvement effort:

1. The manager maintains a list of suggested improvement projects.

2. Periodically, usually quarterly, the manager holds a meeting with his immediate reports to review the list, adding new ones that come up during the meeting and deleting those no longer relevant. This meeting can be part of a regularly scheduled managerial meeting or a separate meeting held for this purpose.

3. The list is then prioritized with the help of the team. This is not a consensus activity; the manager makes the final decision and reviews the list with her manager for concurrence. The manager's manager can help by discussing what other units may be doing on the same subject, thus eliminating duplication of effort.

4. The manager then delegates the top-priority project to a direct report as a task assignment and part of that person's key accountabilities, making sure that adequate resources (such as time, funds, and expert help) are available. It is not just adding another project to someone's already full workload. Delegating a CI project to someone becomes part of that person's task assignments, and something else that person is presently doing may have to be minimized, postponed, or given to another person. Like all task assignments, the format should follow the formula laid out in Path 1, Managerial Planning and Task Assignment, specifying a "what by when."

5. If the project appears large in terms of scope, time, and other resources, the manager may create an ad hoc task force to work on the project, which may likely involve people from other areas. If desired, the manager can appoint someone to

be leader of this temporary project team and report back to the manager on a regular basis.

6. As improvements begin to be implemented, new ones can take their place. There should always be one improvement project under way at all times.

7. On occasion, an improvement project will include the cooperation of another function. Here, the manager needs to work collaboratively with the manager of the other function to achieve an effective outcome. Clarity of the goal and each individual's accountability is critical in this cross-functional endeavor.

Example of a Continual Improvement Meeting

Continual improvement is more than a managerial practice. It's a way of life. W. Somerset Maugham, the great novelist, once wrote, "It is a funny thing about life. If you refuse to accept anything but the best, you very often get it." The opposite is also true. If you go through life accepting the status quo, you'll end up with the ordinary, just "getting by."

CI points the way for you and your team to become extraordinary in a world of the ordinary.

Jennifer: Thanks for setting up this meeting, Ryan. It's good that we all have the opportunity to review the list of possible improvement projects. I have one I'd like to add.

Ryan: Go ahead, Jennifer, that's what this meeting is all about.

Jennifer: Well, it has to do with our selection process, especially the candidate interview and evaluation part. Although the final decision is with management, we in HR handle all of the administration—from preparing role specifications to contacting search organizations, to arranging to bring in candidates for interviews, and so on. It's part of our job, and we've been doing it for years. However, the scheduling of candidates to come in and be interviewed by appropriate managers has never worked well. Emergency meetings, unexpected travel, and other kinds of last-minute schedule changes cause a less-than-professional picture of the overall process. Last week, a candidate arrived, and there was only one manager available to interview her, and that manager was a substitute for someone else. The other two managers who were scheduled for interviews became "unavailable." The substitute manager spent 30 minutes with the candidate, and her evaluation form was only partially filled out. It looks like we'll be bringing that person back again. All this costs extra money and resources.

Ryan: You're right, Jennifer. And with the proposed expansion next year, it'll get worse. Do you think we can improve the process?"

Jennifer: I'm absolutely sure we can. I've been talking to my colleagues in other companies and reading up on some new approaches, and there is much we can do to improve our method.

Ryan: Well, Jennifer, it sounds like we should put this on the list and give it a priority ranking. What do the rest of you think? How long would it take to make some needed changes in our process and what costs might be involved? Frank?

Frank: I've been talking to Jennifer about this. I believe some good candidates have turned us down because of the poor impression we make at the interviews. Other than people's time, there is little cost involved. In fact, we can save money by making the process more efficient and, at the same time, more effective. Jennifer and I think it would take about two months to develop and recommend a revised approach to our selection process.

Ryan: Looks like a winner. If we get approval, we'll need to juggle some assignments around to get this moving. Thanks for that suggestion. Are there any others to add to the list?

CI Checklist

Successful managers:

- ☑ Know that improvement doesn't just happen; it must be a conscious effort.
- ☑ Make CI a part of their accountabilities.
- ☑ Prioritize a list of CI projects, reviewing them on a regular basis.
- ☑ Create an environment where CI suggestions are welcome for consideration.

☑ Conduct periodic meetings on CI with direct reports, bringing up new ideas and allowing participation in the implementation of key projects.

☑ Involve many people from within and outside the unit in CI projects. An ad hoc task force may be needed.

☑ Have at least one CI project under way at all times.

Action Plan

Write down a few things you could do to begin or improve your efforts in this area. Here are some examples:

- At your next management meeting, bring up the subject and ask your direct reports to think about some projects that would be beneficial to implement. Tell them that time will be set aside at the next meeting for discussing and prioritizing a list of key CI projects.

- Have your list ready for this meeting. Discuss each one and ask for suggestions. Use a flipchart or whiteboard to make revisions and add new possible projects.

- Start with one key project that everyone is enthusiastic about.

Afterword

7 Paths to Success

In my consulting experience, there are four critical factors that differentiate the average manager from the outstanding one. They are the foundation of effective management and are covered in this book through the practices described in the 7 Paths. The four factors and their relevant practices are:

1. **Achieving Results**
   Path 1: Managerial Planning and Task Assignment
   Path 2: Managerial Meetings
   Path 3: Context Setting

2. **Developing Employees**
   Path 4: Feedback
   Path 5: Performance Appraisal
   Path 6: Coaching Direct Reports

3. Influencing the Business

Path 1: Task Assignment and Linkage to Strategy

Path 7: Continual Improvement

4. Personal Growth and Effectiveness

The eight self-assessments and action planning

The Practices Calendar (Appendix F)

You are now familiar with the 7 Paths. As a manager, you are probably doing some of the activities that have been covered but not in the depth and detail of the paths described in this book. At this point in your reading, you can make a decision as to the next steps you may wish to take. Here are some options to consider: You can put this book on the shelf and say to yourself, "Well, I learned a few things, and when I have some time, I'll start following one or more of the paths." As we all know, this approach seldom works. The time will never be just right. The thought is well meant but wishing is not a strategy. Hope is not a plan. However, if you don't think you are in your "managerial comfort zone" and that the 7 Paths make sense and fit with where you want to be, then don't wait. Use one of the following two options:

1. Review your self-assessments on the practices contained in the 7 Paths. Start where it is the easiest. For example, you may choose to work on improving something you already have under way, restructure your next management meeting, or review all direct reports' task assignments and convert them to the QQTR format. Start wherever it makes the most sense. But do start.

2. Start where you think you have the most to gain, where the gap between your self-assessment and the ideal is the greatest.

This will give you the highest return on your investment of time and energy.

Practicing the 7 Paths to Managerial Leadership enables the manager to replace poor habits with new, good ones. That is a very effective way to change behavior. Thinking about and developing these new habits will ultimately result in a new and exciting future for you as a manager of others. Keep this Chinese proverb in mind:

Our thoughts become our words.

Our words become our actions.

Our actions become our habits.

Our habits become our character.

Our character becomes our destiny.

As Peter Drucker, the management guru, once said, "Managerial leaders are not made, they are grown." Going down the 7 Paths is an excellent way for a manager to develop into an outstanding managerial leader. Managerial leadership is defined by accomplishing goals, not by possessing certain attributes; by actions, not position power. The 7 Paths will orient your thinking and actions for doing just that. Best wishes in growing into an outstanding managerial leader!

Appendix A

Establishing Key Accountabilities

By Nancy R. Lee and Fred Mackenzie

Key accountabilities (KAs) are the most important assignments a manager gives to each direct report to achieve the unit's goals. Clearly describing each employee's KAs is the crucial step in linking corporate strategy to real-time work output. KAs are actions for which an employee is held accountable. When delegated properly, KAs offer a clear description of what achievements the individual is expected to accomplish within a specific timeframe.

Basic Principles

Assigning key accountabilities and discussing them with each direct report is not a once-a-year exercise. It is a continuing process through which ongoing progress can be gauged of employees' effectiveness in their roles.

KAs include both specific tasks with time constraints and general responsibilities that are ongoing in nature with no specific closure. Together, they define the most important assignments—but not all of them. They are the ones to be focused on during the time period involved. Tasks are an output the manager needs to have completed by a specific time in the future. General responsibilities are outputs that are needed but are ongoing in nature.

There is a distinct difference between position descriptions and key accountabilities. As the name implies, position descriptions cover the activities encompassed in the entire role on an ongoing basis. They are useful in the employment process, developmental planning, and determining role level. Key accountabilities are created by the manager, are time specific, and apply to a specific direct report. They are used as part of the performance appraisal, compensation considerations, and the coaching process. This appendix describes in detail the differences between the two terms.

Managers decide what tasks they will give direct reports. The manager's manager is not to bypass the manager and give assignments, because direct reports are each manager's resources to get the work of the unit done.

Assigning Key Accountabilities

Thinking through the most important work that has to be done in a role and discussing it with a direct report is fundamental to managing. It is this process that helps all employees understand what they are to do. These discussions provide the basis of clarity for employees. Recording the results of these discussions onto a document further defines for both manager and direct report what is expected to happen within a given timeframe.

Not all assignments are key, and some need not be listed. In preparing an accountability document for the person in a role, about four to six assignments are typically identified. This is the most important work to be done within the role in the short term. To achieve full clarity in first-line roles and first-line supervisory roles, it may be necessary to include a few additional KAs.

Key tasks should cover the major thrust of the role for a designated period of time. Typically, 70 to 80 percent of all work would be covered. The priority and list of KAs change from year to year and during the year as well, depending upon overall unit and corporate targets.

Having a clear definition of KAs helps a direct report decide where her time should be spent each day. For this reason, it is also helpful for the manager to list KAs in order of their importance to the unit.

Preparing Key Accountabilities

Key accountabilities should be planned and established by the person's immediate manager. They are then discussed with the direct report for agreement as to the achievability of the assignments, and any needed revisions are made. These KAs are then reviewed by the manager with his manager. The essence of the manager-employee relationship is the clear specification of the KAs to be carried out.

The list should be developed and assigned by the immediate manager to each employee role; this is by far the preferable method. However, sometimes the employee is asked to develop the KAs in draft form for editing and approval by the manager. Although it is not recommended given the time pressure everyone is under, this latter procedure can work provided that the manager does the important tasks of having an initial discussion with the employee on the content, reviewing the draft and changing the list to be compatible with other employees' KAs and, most important, with the manager's own key accountabilities, and reviewing the document with the manager-once-removed for overall consistency.

The final key accountability document should reflect assignments that are challenging, measurable where possible, attainable, and in line with the manager's accountabilities and the corporate goals.

Having the employee actively participate in the process is important for motivation and commitment as well as for clarity of understanding. Employees should feel comfortable asking for clarification on any aspects of the assignment that they do not fully understand.

Assigning Tasks

Managers plan the work of their units and decide what tasks they will give employees to do. They may delegate a task completely to an employee or may assign an employee to assist in one of the manager's own tasks.

Managers decide on and communicate a task (often calling it a goal or project), having in mind an output that is expected to be generated when the task is completed—for example, a report to be written, a research project to be completed, calls on customers to be made, a sale to be closed, a rating to be achieved, a percentage to be reduced, or a meeting to be conducted. Output can be a finite product or a service rendered. Output, whether a product or service, is both visible and observable.

When writing a task assignment, the text should begin with a verb that denotes closure, not one that describes an activity. Some closure verbs are *achieve, complete, conduct, identify, obtain,* and *sell.* Appendix C contains a list of sample closure verbs. Activity verbs—for example, *investigate, analyze, support, assist,* and *monitor*—are not suitable for defining a task. They can, however, be used in describing a general responsibility, which will be discussed later.

In simple terms, a task assignment has three parts: the verb, the subject with metrics when possible, and the timing. Appendix D illustrates the format and gives examples.

QQTR

Key tasks should follow the QQTR format. A task can be defined as a quantity (Q) of things within given quality (Q) limits to be produced by a target completion time (T) within specified resource limits (R).

The manager and direct report can discuss these parameters to agree on an outcome that is satisfactory to the manager and that the employee believes can be accomplished as assigned. This is an important part of the two-way manager-employee working relationship.

QUANTITY (Q)

There is usually a quantity involved in an output, hence the quantity needs to be specified or understood in the assignment of the task. It may be a number, a percentage, or an item, such as a report, proposal, or plan.

Here are some examples of task quantity:

- Reduce air travel by 10 percent in 20xx
- Increase use of online education programs by 20 percent in 20xx
- Conduct x FCS safety drills by 7/1/xxxx.

QUALITY (Q)

The manager specifying output has a quality in mind. There are always quality standards to be met. Too low a quality and the output is unsatisfactory; too high and more resources are used than necessary. The output needs to be provided within certain quality standards, and these standards must be set clearly enough that everyone knows what they are. If an employee is to produce a given quantity to that quality, it is necessary to ensure that the quality needed is understood.

TIME (T)

A task is not only a "what" but is also a "what-by-when"—that which is to be completed by a targeted time. This should be made explicit when assigning a task. The manager plans this target completion time to fit with the other tasks that need to get done to achieve the unit goals.

One of the reasons for making the time explicit when assigning a task is that the employee can discuss with the manager any problems anticipated in meeting the timing, given the resources, quantity, and quality specified. If no target completion time is defined, it is difficult to evaluate task accomplishment.

Tasks can be of any length—for example, a day, a month, six months, a year, 15 months, 18 months, or two years. Too often, managers focus only on what has to be done each year, because appraisals are frequently required to be done annually. It is more effective to think of when the most important tasks need to be completed and then discuss the results with the employee at the time of completion. Tasks of longer than a year in duration can have milestone discussions that help the manager evaluate how things are progressing. The annual appraisal then consists of a review of these completion and milestone discussions and contains no surprises.

RESOURCES (R)

Tasks need to be assigned in terms of existing resources—for example, the amount of money that can be spent, how many worker-hours can be used, or what equipment and materials are available. The resources that are available are often not explicitly discussed, but the manager must ensure that the employee understands what they are because resources directly affect the other three parameters (quantity, quality, and time). The employee should be clear about what resources are available and negotiate available resources with the manager if there are concerns.

An example of QQTR is a report that needs to be written. The manager sets the context by describing to the employee why the report is needed, the topic of the report, and an overview of the literature search that needs to be carried out, resulting in a survey of at least 80 percent of all identified writing on the subject published during the last two years. This provides both the quantity and quality expected and a way to consider how effective the employee was in completing the task.

The manager states that the researcher has three months to complete the report (time). The manager tells the employee, for example, that there is a budget of $1,500 to cover research expenses and that an intern will be provided to help compile the bibliography (resources). The manager expects the employee to work on this report, along with other ongoing work, in such a way that the report will be completed on time, as will all of the employee's other assigned tasks.

Policies and Procedures

Although quality standards, policy, and procedure limits are not always explicitly stated, they always exist and are implicitly assumed by both manager and direct report. It is a manager's responsibility to familiarize direct reports with these and see that they are adhered to in working on tasks. This is critically important with policies that involve safety or legal liability.

Prioritization and Changing Circumstances

The manager sets priorities for the work of direct reports. Where possible, it is useful to list key tasks in order of priority, adding additional clarity to the document. When a direct report is not able to complete a task as defined, he should go to the manager in time for adjustments to be made. This is often caused by a change in circumstances or prevailing conditions. When this occurs, the direct report goes to the manager to discuss the situation and, when possible, makes suggestions as to changes that might be made. It is the manager who then makes the decisions and reprioritizes, often adjusting the QQTR of that or other tasks. The goal is to have all tasks completed to QQTR with no unpleasant surprises for the manager.

If There Is Need for Speed

Both managers and direct reports generally have a good idea of what is a reasonable time needed to complete an assignment. If the manager assigns a task that is to be completed in three months, it is a different task than if the direct report is given one month to do it. Some people have difficulty with this point and think that it cannot be a different task just because the time allowed is two months less—but it is a different task. The direct report will have to make different decisions and behave differently. The manager may have to adjust some of the other parameters, such as quality or quantity, and perhaps assign more resources, or revise the direct report's other tasks.

With only one month to do the report, the direct report may decide to do much less research, and the literature review may have to be much more cursory. The employee will have to decide to adjust the work she has to do on other tasks in quite a different way because of the allotted time she has been given to complete the report.

Depending upon how much time the direct report has to spend on the report, she will have to consider what can be set aside for now and what cannot, while still completing all of the assignments on time. Where these decisions affect other key assignments, the direct report will need to discuss these issues with the manager. It is the manager who adjusts some of those other assignments if the report must be finished in a relatively unrealistic time period.

For example, the direct report, who now must complete the report very quickly, may ask the manager for temporary clerical help to be assigned to assist with certain aspects of producing the report and ask to have the date on another task postponed for several weeks.

What—Not How

In establishing key tasks, it is neither necessary nor desirable to describe how to accomplish the task. That is for the direct report to decide and is part of his work. As long as the work of direct reports remains within the boundaries set by the organization, allowing them to get on with their responsibilities in their own way is what is empowering, creative, and rewarding for them. When a manager describes how to do a task in great detail (micromanaging), it may indicate:

- The direct report may not be of the right level to do the work of the role.
- Coaching the direct report is required to help her grow in the job.
- The manager may not know how or be hesitant to delegate (fear of failure).

An example of too much "how":

By working with the business units, discussing their concerns, and reviewing the last five years of statistical data, create charts on an Excel spreadsheet and analyze trends to determine future actions regarding the avoidable and unavoidable turnover situation. After reviewing the results with the business units, revise and submit a report with recommendations by 10/31/xxxx.

Although the manager and direct report may wish to discuss some of the methods to be used, the task might be stated more simply:

By 10/31/xxxx, submit a report on the present status of employee turnover rate and recommend actions to be taken to reduce future avoidable turnover.

General Responsibilities

As mentioned, ongoing key accountabilities are called general responsibilities. General responsibilities are closer to the things typically described in position descriptions. They do not have a deadline for completion. However, they occasionally have specific tasks embedded in them that have related target dates involved.

General responsibilities:

- are typically limited to the four or five most important (key)
- directly relate to the goals of the unit and the strategy of the organization
- are specific to the role (not universal items, such as control the budget, build the team, support the strategy, develop direct reports, or manage the unit).

Sometimes it is desirable to include certain generic statements as part of every direct report's key accountability document to support legal requirements or place emphasis on a particular concern, such as safety.

When writing a general responsibility statement, begin with an action verb, such as *monitor, oversee, provide, participate, maintain, assist,* or *support.* Here are some examples of a general responsibility statement:

- Revise the company organization charts each time there is a change in personnel.

- Remain current with changes in the OSHA regulations regarding _____.
- Serve on the following committees: _____.
- When changes occur, update the policy and procedures manual quarterly except for safety issues, which need to be distributed within one week of approval.

Summary

The foundation of the manager-direct report relationship is the clear specification of the employee's key accountabilities. Clarity in the most important assignments, both key tasks and key general responsibilities, is critical to enhancing trust and achieving the overall success of the organization.

Appendix B

Employee Document Comparisons

The following table shows the difference between a position description, which describes the role in general, and a key accountability document, which provides specific assignments from the manager to the person in the role.

Table B-1: Employee Document Comparisons

Document Element	Position Description	Key Accountability Document
Scope	Everything in Role	Key assignments for specific time period
Origin	Human Resources	Managers' accountabilities for specified period of time

Table B-1: Employee Document Comparisons (continued)

Document Element	Position Description	Key Accountability Document
Strategy	Not Related	Supports and aligned with the corporate strategy
Description	Activities	QQTR
Updating	Seldom	Often, somtimes, twice a year
Performance	Not Related	Basis of appraisal
Utilization	Passive	Dynamic
Verbs	Open Ended	Closure
Time	Ongoing	Specific and varies with assignment

Note: It is possible for two incumbents with the same role specifications (position description) to have different key accountability documents for the same time period.

Appendix C

Sample Closure Verbs

Table C-1: Sample Closure Verbs

Key Closure Verbs	Also Usable	Usable With Added Closure Verbs
Achieve	Appraise	Advise and . . .
Audit	Approve	Analyze and . . .
Close	Assign	Apply and . . .
Complete	Attend	Arrange and . . .
Conduct	Authorize	Assure and . . .
Consolidate	Classify	Check and . . .
Eliminate	Construct	Consolidate and . . .
Establish	Create	Describe and . . .
Evaluate	Deliver	Determine and . . .
Generate	Design	Develop and . . .
Identify	Distribute	Inspect and . . .

Table C-1: Sample Closure Verbs (continued)

Key Closure Verbs	Also Usable	Usable With Added Closure Verbs
Implement	Execute	Interview and . . .
Initiate	Issue	Perform and . . .
Manage	Open	Prepare and . . .
Obtain	Provide	Review and . . .
Recommend	Select	Revise and . . .
Schedule	Summarize	Transmit and . . .
Sell	Test	Update and . . .
Submit	Train	Verify and . . .

Appendix D

Assignment Examples

Table D-1: Assignment Examples

Closure Verb	Metrics, Subject	Completion Date
Execute	newly approved XX plan	by 7/31/xxxx
Submit	recommendations for XX	by 8/31/xxxx
Reduce	avoidable turnover by 20 percent compared with average for the years 20xx-20yy	by 12/31/xxxx
Increase	20xx customer satisfaction ratings by 15 percent over 20yy	by 12/31/xxxx
Implement	two LEAN process reviews and submit results	first by 7/31/xxxx second by 11/30/xxxx

Table D-1: Assignment Examples (continued)

Closure Verb	Metrics, Subject	Completion Date
Achieve	profit of minimum $200K from P&S projects	by 12/31/xxxx
Conduct	CPI/LEAN training to 50 percent of total workforce	by 11/15/xxxx
Provide	up-to-date budget information to XXX for use in managing the budget throughout the year	

Appendix E

Making Strategy Work—The Linkage Process

By Nancy R. Lee and Fred Mackenzie

The linkage process is a method of converting an organization's long-term plans into actual work output. It involves a logical and systematic procedure in which employees, at all levels, actively participate.

There are two compelling reasons for implementing this process. The first is organizational, and the second is individual. Organizationally, it establishes a step-by-step way of ensuring that long-range plans and objectives are translated into desired results. Individually, it creates understanding of how each employee's work output contributes to the overall goals of the organization. This enhances the motivation of each person, because output becomes personal-goal accomplishment, not just ongoing day-to-day activity.

Aligning individual assignments with organizational objectives is a win-win opportunity. It is both logical and essential that the sum total of the employee's work achieves the overall objectives of the organization. The better the fit between work output and corporate strategy, the more outstanding the results, in which the ordinary becomes the extraordinary. Agreeing with this conclusion is easy. Implementing it takes effort.

For objectivity and skill in facilitating the linkage process, it is helpful that an external consultant be used, at least for the initial cycle. There are four steps that lay the foundation to achieve linkage between corporate objectives and employee assignments.

Step 1: Establish a Plan

As in life itself, little progress on anticipated results can be made without first having a mission and a plan.

Having a strategic plan is the first step in the linkage process. It typically begins with senior management determining and then communicating the organization's values, vision, mission, and overall strategy.

With the long-range strategy in place, senior management meets to decide to focus on four to six key factors that will make the difference in whether the organization is successful or not. These are called critical success factors (CSFs). They are subjects, not action phrases.

Typical examples are growth, profitability, technology, human resources, manufacturing, acquisitions and divestitures, access to capital, and product development.

Step 2: Create Corporate Objectives

Each of the identified CSFs is broken down into long-range corporate objectives, typically with either a three- or five-year horizon. If doing this for the first time, three years may be the most effective to use. There are usually about four objectives for each CSF. Here, numbers, percentages, milestone, dates, and other metrics are included. These are organizational objectives; individual accountabilities are not delineated at this time.

The formulation of these long-range corporate objectives is generally accomplished in a meeting of senior management, where the group is divided into subgroups working within the CSF of their expertise. The findings of the subgroups are then shared with the larger group for understanding and modification. This activity should result in 16 to 24 corporate objectives, which all of senior management has participated in formulating. The role of the CEO in this process is paramount, because he will be held accountable for the end results. This is an example of a corporate objective: Complete two acquisitions within three years, one in the United States and one in Europe.

Step 3: Develop Short-Term Goals

From these corporate objectives, short-term goals are developed. These are usually 12 to 18 months in duration. On average, there are about three to five short-term goals for each of the long-range objectives, yielding anywhere from 50 to 100 corporate short-term goals.

To determine these short-term goals, senior managment decides who should work on creating them for each of the corporate objectives. Teams are created to address each of the objectives. Each team develops specific goals from the objective (or objectives) assigned to them and submits the draft to a planning facilitator for consolidation into a list of goals by CSF and objective. All goals are assigned to a functional manager, who is accountable for achieving the goal. This list is then distributed to all members of senior management for review prior to meeting as a group.

A group meeting is held to discuss, clarify, and modify as necessary the corporate short-term goals. This meeting may include members of the working teams who are not part of senior management. It is important not to have more goals than senior management believes can be accomplished during the designated timeframe.

The end result is a master corporate document showing corporate short-term goals, how they relate to long-term corporate objectives, and the critical success factors derived from the strategy.

Here is an example of a corporate short-term goal: Within 18 months, identify four potential acquisitions, two in the United States and two in Europe.

Senior management has now participated in formulating, developing, and understanding the organization's specific goals for the near term as well as the long-term objectives. The process has now moved from the strategic (planning) stage to the tactical (operational) stage.

Step 4: Establish Individual Key Accountabilities

The last step in this process is the linkage of short-term corporate objectives and goals to individual accountabilities. The CEO works with her direct reports individually to determine their key accountabilities. Many times, a corporate short-term goal (and sometimes a corporate long-term objective) becomes the key accountability for one of the CEO's direct reports, who, in turn, delegates all or part of it to his own direct reports. It then gets broken down into task assignments for directors, managers, and so forth as the assignments cascade throughout the organization.

Some education is required at the beginning of Step 4 for proper crafting of the key accountabilities (important task assignments) by the managers at all levels. This would include the use of a customized key accountabilities document, which sets out a road map for each employee's work output for a given time period.

This is an example of a key accountability: Within six months, establish an acquisition task force, have members agree on a plan to proceed, and submit this plan to the CEO for approval.

Conclusion

The foundation of the linkage process is the clarity of individual accountabilities as they cascade throughout the organization. Managers delegate task assignments to specific direct reports based on corporate goals and objectives.

The secret of the effectiveness of this process is in the ability of managers to determine appropriate accountabilities, explain these task assignments to their direct reports so that they understand what needs to be done, and then to allow the employees latitude to craft the actions necessary to complete them. The participation of direct reports is not in determining their accountabilities but in deciding how they will be achieved.

Linking long-range strategy to individual key accountabilities (Figure E-1) transforms broad strategic plans into focused operational plans in which all employees understand and feel part of the overall direction and thrust of the organization, both in the short term and long term.

Figure E-1: Linking Strategy to Results

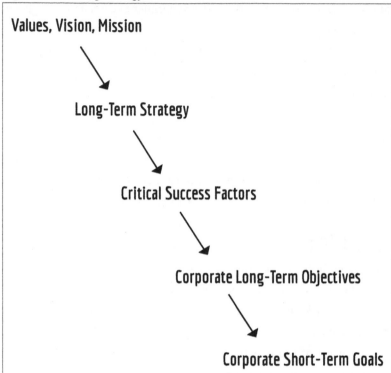

Appendix F

Using the Practices Calendar

As you become familiar with the 7 Paths to Managerial Leadership, you will need a plan to get started and maintain momentum. This is where the managerial leadership practices calendar comes in handy.

On the next page is an example of a completed calendar. As you can see, it is laid out with the 12 months of the year across the top and the 7 Paths down the side. Various letters allow planning by month and by practice. In this example, the manager:

- scheduled three context-setting meetings during the year (in conjunction with three managerial meetings)
- scheduled two performance appraisal meetings with each direct report (informal midyear and formal at year-end)
- scheduled a number of individual coaching sessions with different employees

- included monthly reminders to give feedback to employees
- scheduled periodic meetings with all direct reports on the status of their key task assignments
- scheduled managerial meetings on problem solving and other issues
- scheduled periodic meetings to assess the key continual improvement projects.

As items are accomplished, they can be crossed off in red, which offers a visual image of progress being made.

The completed calendar gives the manager an overall look at the current year, what has been accomplished, and what has not been done in terms of the managerial leadership practice.

Path	Jan	Feb	Mar	Apr	May	Jun	Jul	Aug	Sept	Oct	Nov	Dec
Task Assignment	T			T			T			T		
Managerial Meetings	M		M		M			M		M		
Context Setting	X				X					X		
Feedback	F	F	F	F	F	F	F	F	F	F	F	F
Appraisal						A						A
Coaching	C						C			C		
Continual Improvement			I			I			I		I	

X = Context-Setting Meeting   A = Performance Appraisals
C = Coaching Session   F = Feedback Reminders
T = Task Assignment Status   M = Managerial Meetings
I = Continual Improvement Review

Glossary

7 Paths: The critical paths leading to superior managerial leadership.

Accountabilities (key): These are the most important task assignments and general responsibilities given to an employee; they account for about 80 percent of the person's output.

Appraisal: Periodic discussions of the manager's judgment of a direct report's effectiveness; the annual appraisal summarizes these discussions.

Authority: The power vested in a person by virtue of her role to expend resources: financial, material, technical, and human.

Calendar of practices: A 12-month planning map indicating actions to be taken on the 7 Paths to Managerial Leadership.

Closure verbs: Verbs that describe completion when writing a task assignment.

Coaching: Assisting a direct report to (a) handle a task in his role more effectively and (b) understand the full scope of the role and be able to fill it more completely.

Context setting: Regular updating of the bigger picture within which an employee's work is carried out.

Counseling: Directed toward behavioral problems (alcohol, drugs, or other health issues, for example) affecting work output, normally done by outside specialists.

Courage: The ability for the manager and the direct report to speak frankly to each other (adult to adult) on important issues without fear of negative consequences.

Decision: The making of a choice with the commitment of resources.

Delegation: The act of assigning a task to a direct report.

Direct report: A person who reports directly to the manager with no one in between.

Feedback (positive and constructive): Praising an employee when something good was accomplished (positive) and telling an employee when results are not up to expectations (constructive).

Feedback reminders: Developing a habit of using the feedback process with direct reports through the use of symbols, methods, and techniques.

Filter (human forces): The many factors that distort an employee's work behavior away from what is theoretically expected.

General responsibilities: That portion of an employee's account-abilities that are ongoing in nature.

Improvement (continual): Part of the manager's accountability to seek out and implement improvement projects within her control. For example, this can be a process, a system, or a procedure.

Linkage process: Through a series of steps, the process of aligning individual key accountabilities and work output to the long-term strategy and goals of the organization.

Manager: A person in a role in which he is held accountable not only for his own personal effectiveness but also for the work of direct reports.

Managerial leadership: Combines the discipline of managing a unit with the skill of enabling employees to work at their level of capability.

Managerial leadership practices: The 7 Paths covered in this book.

Managerial meetings: Regular meetings with direct reports involving two-way information sharing on a variety of subjects.

Managerial planning: The manager's determination of task assignments.

Mentoring: The helping of an employee in formulating her future plans beyond the present role by someone higher in the organization.

Organizational structure: A system of roles and role relationships that people are given when they work together. These role relationships establish the boundaries within which people relate to one another.

Output: A product or service produced in a given period of time—a completion of an assigned task.

Project team: An ad hoc group of individuals brought together under a team leader to complete a specific assignment.

QQTR: When formulating task assignments, quality, quantity, completion time, and resources available should be described and understood.

Role: Another name for a position or job.

Role specification: Different from the traditional job description, this document spells out the specific key accountabilities of the role, both tasks and general responsibilities, not just the activities and qualifications.

Self-assessments: An opportunity for the reader to judge his present proficiencies on the various managerial leadership practices covered in this book.

Silo effect: When work of one group is isolated from another and communication is essentially vertical and not horizontal; also known as stovepiping.

Skill: An ability (learned through training, practice, and experience) to carry out a given procedure without having to think through the steps involved; sometimes labeled "unconscious competence."

Task assignments: Assigning a task to produce a specified output and describing it using QQTR (see QQTR).

Teaching: A general term describing the activity of transferring knowledge or skill to someone else.

Training: The process of improving performance in one or more aspects of an employee's work output through additional knowledge and or skill.

Unit: Any group of people working together toward a common goal with an accountable manager. For example, it could be a section, department, or function.

Work: The exercise of judgment and discretion in making decisions and carrying out goal-oriented activities.

Work planning: The planning by the manager of the work that has to be done, by whom, by when, and how best to use available resources.

References

Introduction

Jaques, E. 2006. *Requisite Organization: A Total System for Effective Managerial Organization and Managerial Leadership for the 21st Century*, rev. ed. Gloucester, MA: Cason Hall.

Lee, N.R. 2007. *The Practice of Managerial Leadership*. Xlibris.

Chapter 1

Harter, J., and A. Adkins. 2015. "Employees Want a Lot More From Their Managers." *Gallup Business Journal*, April 8. www.gallup.com/businessjournal/182321/emplo-yees-lot-managers.aspx.

Chapter 9

Lee, N.R. 2007. *The Practice of Managerial Leadership*. Xlibris.

Managerial Leadership Practices

For those readers who wish to learn more about managerial leadership practices and the concepts underlying them, the following books are suggested:

Burns, G. 2012. *A Is for Accountability: A Guide to Accountability-Based Management*. Bloomington, IN: Trafford.

Capelle, R.G. 2013. *Optimizing Organizational Design: A Proven Approach to Enhance Financial Performance, Customer Satisfaction, and Employee Engagement*. San Francisco: Jossey-Bass.

Charan, R., S. Drotter, and J. Noel. 2010. *The Leadership Pipeline: How to Build the Leadership Powered Company*, 2nd ed. San Francisco: Jossey-Bass.

Clement, S.D., and C.R. Clement. 2013. *It's All About Work: Organizing Your Company to Get Work Done*.

Conaty, B., and R. Charan. 2010. *The Talent Masters: Why Smart Leaders Put People Before Numbers*. New York: Crown Business.

De Visch, J. 2010. *The Vertical Dimension: Blueprint to Align Business and Talent Development*. Mechelen, Belgium: Connect & Transform Press.

Dive, B. 2004. *The Healthy Organization: A Revolutionary Approach to People & Management*, 2nd ed. Sterling, VA: Kogan Page.

Jaques, E. 2002. *Social Power and the CEO: Leadership and Trust in a Sustainable Free Enterprise System*. Westport, CT: Quorum.

Kraines, G. 2011. *Accountability Leadership: How to Strengthen Productivity Through Sound Managerial Leadership*. Pompton Plains, NJ: Career Press.

Macdonald, I., C. Burke, and K. Stewart. 2012. *Systems Leadership: Creating Positive Organisations*. Burlington, VT: Gower.

About the Author

Fred Mackenzie has decades of experience as an executive with Mobil Oil; Training House, a major publisher of instructional programs and assessments; and MLI, a contract manufacturer for GE, Kodak, and IBM. His consulting experience is in three major areas: managerial leadership, succession planning, and strategic planning.

During his time with Mobil Oil, he served as a manager in organization development, management education, and training consulting systems, and as a senior consultant. He held various human resource management roles in Africa, the Middle East, and Europe and was CEO of International Management Consultants, a European-based consortium of management consultants operating in Europe, Africa, and the Middle East.

Fred has undergraduate degrees in psychology and geological engineering, master's degrees in personnel psychology and micropaleontology, and a PhD in psychology. He is listed in *Who's Who in America* and *Who's Who in the World*.

Fred has served on the faculty of Cornell University's advanced management program, Oxford University's Institute for Advanced Managerial Studies, and Henley Management College, UK.